£1·50

# Older and Wiser

A Study of Educational Provision for
Black and Ethnic Minority Elders

Stella Dadzie

D1351086

**EUROPEAN YEAR**
OF OLDER PEOPLE AND
SOLIDARITY BETWEEN GENERATIONS
**1993**

# NIACE
THE NATIONAL ORGANISATION
FOR ADULT LEARNING

*Published by the National Institute of Adult Continuing Education*
*21 De Montfort Street, Leicester LE1 7GE*

Company registration number 2603322
Charity number 1002775

*First published 1993*

**Cataloguing in Publication Data**
*A CIP record for this title is available from the British Library*

*ISBN 1 872941 48 6*

*Printed and bound in Great Britain by The Cromwell Press, Wilts.*

# Acknowledgements

I am very grateful to Jenny Martin, whose interviews and research into provision for black elders in Leicestershire provided the basis for the Leicester Case Studies.

Thanks also to the many individuals who have given us their valuable time and insight during the course of this research project. Their readiness to complete lengthy questionnaires, to act as interpreters, and to invite us into the different projects to meet with clients and discuss their work has made this report possible.

Particular thanks should go to:

Chetin Ahmet (Turkish-Cypriot Elders Project, Haringey)
Norita Bahra (Living History Project, Leicester)
Mrs Delomi Caleb (Highfields Youth and Community Centre)
Nidia Castro (Development Worker for Elderly Refugees/
    British Refugee Council)
Mrs C. (Avalon Community Education Project)
Mrs Diwaliben (Rushey Mead Language Centre)
Ben Gamadia (Age Concern, Leicester)
Mrs Grant (South Fields Open Workshop)
David Idiabana and Theresa (The Pepperpot Club)
Bob Johnson, Vera Johnson, Beth Morgan and Olwyn Watkins
    (Butetown History and Arts Project)
Mrs Kashiben (Rushy Mead Language Centre)
Mr Udham Singh Mahal (Wesley Hall Community Project)
Mrs Mariben (Rushey Mead Language Centre)
Carlos Mesa (Latin American Third Age Project)
Jasbir Panesar (Asian Elders Video Project)
Mina Patel (Ethnic Minorities Liaison Officer, Age Concern)
Razia Shamim (Age Concern, Metro Rochdale)
Mr Karnail Singh (Wesley Hall Community Project)
Amada Vergara, Anna and Hermosina (Latin American
    Golden Years Project)
Maxine Warren (Age Concern, Newcastle-upon-Tyne)

# Background

The Older and Wiser project was commissioned by NIACE in support of the European Year of the Older Adult and Solidarity Between Generations. The project was short-term and involved three key stages:

## Research

A number of areas with a significant black elderly population were identified for action research purposes between April and July 1993. These included:

- Brixton, London Borough of Lambeth
- Butetown, Cardiff
- Ladbroke Grove, London Borough of Kensington and Chelsea
- Leicester
- Newcastle-upon-Tyne
- Southall, London Borough of Ealing
- Tottenham, London Borough of Haringey.

Targeting criteria included:

- the need to provide a representative sample of responses within both the statutory and voluntary sectors
- the need to demonstrate the diversity of educational needs within the elderly populations of different black (i.e. African/Caribbean/Asian/refugee) communities
- the need to highlight a range of possible responses to the learning needs and aspirations of elderly black people.

Over 50 organisations and individuals involved in this area of work were contacted (see Appendix 1). A number of projects appearing to meet the criteria were selected and invited to provide information about their work with elderly black clients. Some were subsequently visited for the purpose of interviewing participants, project co-ordinators and tutors, as appropriate. Interviews were based on a set of standard questions, covering the origins, status, aims, rationale and effectiveness of their provision and the educational and other benefits to their clients (see Appendix 3).

## Interim report

An interim verbal report was produced for a NIACE conference held during Adult Learners' Week in May 1993, providing a brief overview of the findings to date and some of the lessons for statutory and voluntary providers seeking to meet the needs of older black people (see Appendix 2).

## Report for publication

This publication is the outcome of the project, and is based on research completed between April and August 1993. It sets out to provide some examples of the excellent work being done with black elders, both as an illustration of good practice in the provision of educational opportunities for older black people, and as a rationale for its development.

It is hoped that the information and case studies which follow will prove relevant not only to providers in the UK who are seeking to expand their services to the black elderly but also to those in the wider European Community.

# Who are the Black Elderly?

The focus of this report is the growing population of older members of black and 'ethnic minority' communities – those people over the age of 50 who belong to settled communities; and those who came to Britain as migrants, immigrants or refugees and now find themselves facing old age and retirement in this country.

Although they are not all black in terms of skin-colour, they are all potential targets of racism because of their identifiable racial, national, ethnic, religious, cultural or linguistic differences. The term 'black' is therefore used throughout this publication as a convenient umbrella term, and includes African, Caribbean, Asian, Chinese, Turkish-Cypriot, Latin American and other elderly people who are not members of the ethnic majority.

## What do they have in common?

Despite the varying individual circumstances which brought their communities here, and the range of needs and perspectives represented within them, older black people have much in common. Many will have come to Britain through necessity rather than through choice, in search of work or education, or as a result of conditions of political or economic desperation. All of them will have experienced the traumas of uprooting and of learning to survive in an unfamiliar, unwelcoming environment. Many have also experienced the horrors of poverty, war, victimisation or torture and the grief of losing their homes, children and loved ones.

Some black elders are relatively fortunate, in that they have family and communities around them who can appreciate their needs and speak their languages. Others are lonely and isolated and may be heavily dependent on less than adequate local services. Far too often, whether dependent or not, there is a lack of suitable provision catering for their social, cultural, religious, dietary, linguistic, health and learning needs – and a reluctance or inability to ask.

In such a context, it is easy to overlook the wealth of experience, skills and resourcefulness that characterises these groups of elderly people. There is no doubt that, because of the harsh conditions which have shaped their working lives and their lack of access to available services due to language barriers and institutional racism, their needs are considerable. However, they have not always been dependent on others to meet them. Many come from a long tradition of self-reliance which, to the detriment of the wider community, still remains largely unrecognised and untapped.

The case studies in this report demonstrate clearly that, given the funds, premises and resources, elderly black people are more than capable of identifying their own learning needs and finding innovative ways of improving the quality of their own lives. They also confirm that, however informal and however loosely defined, education can benefit people of all ages and is not the prerogative of the young and able-bodied.

# The Black Elderly in Britain: An Overview

The 1991 Census has provided the first comprehensive overview of the numbers of elderly black and ethnic minority people living in Britain. Among the many important demographic findings from a recent analysis of the data conducted by Warwick University's Centre for Research in Ethnic Relations are a number of revelations which can actively assist providers in their efforts to plan for future provision for elderly black clients:

- in 1991 there were just over 3 million black people from ethnic minorities living in Great Britain, 164,306 of whom were aged 65 or over
- black and ethnic minority communities tend to be considerably younger than the indigenous white community, with children under 15 making up a third of the black/ethnic minority population, compared to a fifth of the white population
- while 16% of the population as a whole is now aged over 65, only 3.2% of the black/ethnic minority population falls within this age group
- this figure, though comparatively small, represents an increase in the 65+ age group of 168.5%, when compared to their estimated numbers in 1981
- there are some significant variations in the age structure of the different communities – for example, amongst those of black African origin, elderly Caribbeans comprise 5.65% of their community, compared to 1.48% of elderly Africans
- although African-Caribbeans represent the largest group of black elderly in this country, the overall African-Caribbean population has declined by -14% over the past 10 years; this compares with an increase in the total Bangladeshi population of +144%; total African (+88%); total Pakistani (+71%) and total Mixed Race/Other (+157%)
- black/ethnic minority groups have a lower ratio of young and elderly dependents than the white population
- amongst all ethnic minority groups, there are currently 15.18% between the ages of 45 and 64; this represents a huge increase in the numbers of black elderly people who will be in need of appropriate provision over the coming two decades

- over the next 30 to 40 years, the percentage of elderly black people is set to increase tenfold – 3.22% rising to 32.49%.

*The above data are based on findings from the 1991 Census Statistical Paper No 2 (University of Warwick Centre for Research in Ethnic Relations, February 1993).*

# Ethnic Minority Groups by Age

A breakdown of ethnic groups by age, based on the 1991 Census, shows significant fluctuations in the numbers of elders in the different communities who are aged 65 or over, and those who will be reaching retirement age over the next 20 years:

**Age breakdown of ethnic groups in Great Britain, 1991**

| Ethnic Group | Total Population | Percentage of total population | | | | | |
|---|---|---|---|---|---|---|---|
| | | Aged 0-4 | Aged 5-15 | Aged 16-24 | Aged 25-44 | Aged 45-64 | Aged 65+ |
| White | 51,873.80 | 6.36 | 12.97 | 12.55 | 29.01 | 22.32 | 16.80 |
| All ethnic minorities | 3,015.10 | 11.10 | 21.94 | 16.06 | 32.49 | 15.18 | 3.22 |
| Black | 890.70 | 11.12 | 18.28 | 16.11 | 33.27 | 17.43 | 3.79 |
| Black - Caribbean | 500.00 | 7.56 | 14.33 | 14.87 | 32.74 | 24.85 | 5.65 |
| Black - African | 212.40 | 11.83 | 17.51 | 16.61 | 42.17 | 10.40 | 1.48 |
| Black - Other | 178.40 | 20.28 | 30.27 | 19.01 | 24.18 | 4.97 | 1.29 |
| South Asian | 1,479.60 | 10.89 | 24.82 | 16.19 | 30.21 | 14.89 | 2.99 |
| Indian | 840.30 | 8.81 | 20.74 | 15.19 | 34.61 | 16.60 | 4.06 |
| Pakistani | 476.60 | 13.13 | 29.52 | 17.47 | 25.79 | 12.35 | 1.73 |
| Bangladeshi | 162.80 | 15.06 | 32.17 | 17.60 | 20.46 | 13.51 | 1.20 |
| Chinese and others | 644.70 | 11.57 | 20.39 | 15.70 | 36.65 | 12.72 | 2.98 |
| Chinese | 156.90 | 7.09 | 16.25 | 17.86 | 41.17 | 14.25 | 3.38 |
| Other Asians | 197.50 | 8.02 | 16.39 | 14.72 | 43.48 | 15.04 | 2.36 |
| Other – Other | 290.20 | 16.40 | 25.34 | 15.20 | 29.55 | 10.31 | 3.20 |
| **Entire Population** | **54,888.80** | **6.62** | **13.46** | **12.74** | **29.20** | **21.93** | **16.05** |

Source: 1991 Census Local Base Statistics (ESRC purchase); Crown Copyright

*Source: 1991 Census Statistical Paper No 2 (University of Warwick Centre for Research in Ethnic Relations, February 1993).*

# Population Pyramids

The following Population Pyramids provide a useful overview of the age and gender structures of individual black/ethnic minority populations. The extent of diversity represented here, both in terms of age and family structures and the different social, educational, cultural and linguistic aspirations that exist between and within each community, should need no emphasis.

# Population Pyramids for individual ethnic groups

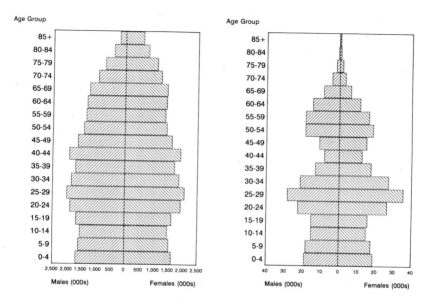

Figure 1: White people

Figure 2: Black-Caribbeans

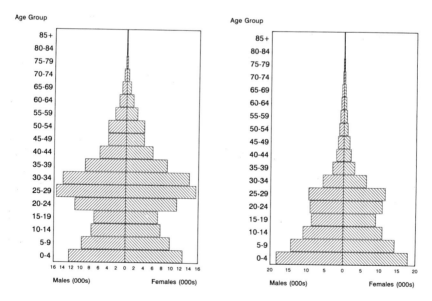

Figure 3: Black-Africans

Figure 4: Black-Others

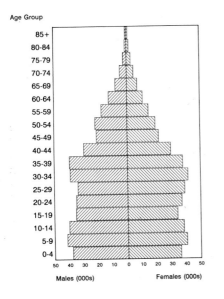

Figure 5: Indians

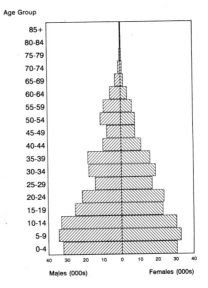

Figure 6: Pakistanis

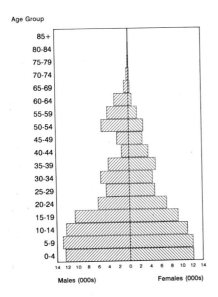

Figure 7: Bangladeshis

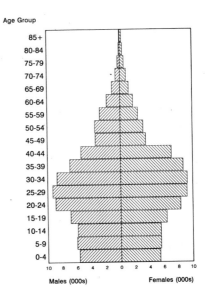

Figure 8: Chinese

Age Group

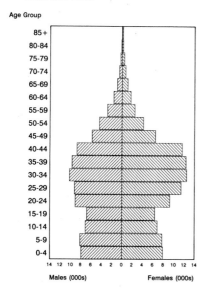

Figure 9: Other-Asians

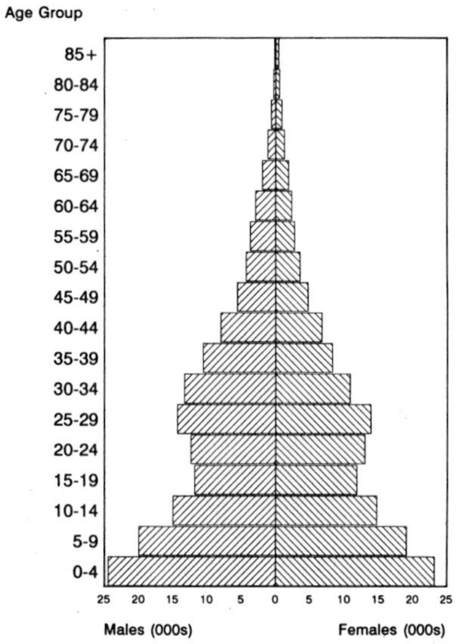

Age Group

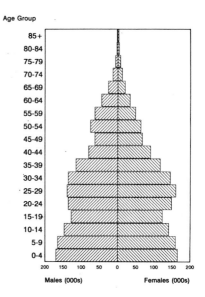

Figure 10: Other-Others

Age Group

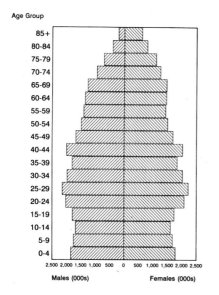

Figure 11: Entire Population

Age Group

Figure 12: Ethnic Minorities

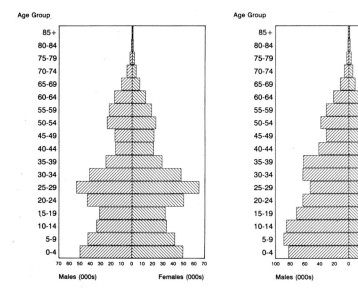

Figure 13: Black People        Figure 14: South Asians

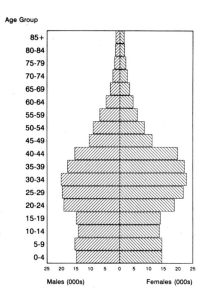

Figure 15: Chinese and Others

Source: *1991 Census Statistical Paper No 2 (University of Warwick's Centre for Research in Ethnic Relations, February 1993).*

17

# African-Caribbean Elders

African-Caribbean elders are currently the largest and most visible group of black elderly in this country. Those over 65 make up 5.65% of a community of 500,000, while the 45–64 age-group stands at 24.85%. These numbers – and their implications for providers of post-retirement services – cannot be ignored.

Despite having spent much of their working lives in England, many elderly African-Caribbeans do not relish the prospect of living out their retirement in this country, and still cling to the dream of returning home. The 14% reduction in the overall African-Caribbean community is at least in part due to the exodus of older people who, having raised their children and reached the age of retirement, are now free to leave.

For those who cannot exercise such a choice, the experience of old age is likely to be very different from the life they might have anticipated 'back home'. A study of African-Caribbean elders in Nottinghamshire in 1981[1] revealed that many experienced loneliness, cultural and social isolation and a sense of 'being on the scrap-heap' despite the proximity of a relatively settled community. Over a third of those interviewed either had no living relatives or had children who were living overseas.

A long history of self-reliance and regular employment meant that they felt ill-prepared for increasing dependency into old age, whether this was because of immobility, infirmity or poverty. Yet over half of the Nottingham respondents were claiming Supplementary Benefits and a similar number were living in council accommodation.

Other findings from this study, and two other studies conducted by AFFOR (All Faiths for One Race) and Age Concern[2] revealed that:

- the majority of African-Caribbean elders are likely to have lived in this country for between 30 years or more
- many will have lived in the same city or neighbourhood for 10 years or more

- like other groups of immigrants, they have tended to settle in the inner-cities either because of better employment prospects or to be close to others from their island or region
- the dispersal of children and high rates of continued migration have led to a weakening of traditional family and community support structures for the elderly
- many African-Caribbean pensioners receive lower pensions than their white counterparts
- many also experience institutional racism and individual acts of prejudice, leading to a desire for more day-care facilities of their own.

A tendency to lump 'West Indians' together has led to a lack of awareness of their cultural diversity. As Alison Norman points out,[3]

> 'it is important to remember that there are very distinct differences in language, culture and previous experience between people from different parts of the Caribbean, and that someone whose homeland may be 1000 miles away from that of a fellow 'West Indian' may have little in common with him (sic). People from a particular island do tend to settle together ... but even if the population in a particular area is relatively homogeneous, there will be exceptions, and it is important, in terms of service provision, that awareness of the plurality of West Indian culture is maintained.'

The potential isolation of elders from the Caribbean community has been considerably reduced thanks to the important role of black church organisations in providing them with a social, cultural and educational focus. However, these benefits are restricted to churchgoers. As the first generation of post-war settlers with active Church ties is gradually replaced by people who have spent their substantial lives in Britain and who may have less church involvement, it is clear that other agencies will have an increasing role to play.

In the course of this research, it was evident that many elderly African-Caribbeans have already ventured into the mainstream of provision, through adult education classes, voluntary projects, social clubs and day centres. However, they have often done so at the risk of isolation and discrimination. With the projected growth in the number of elders, there is a pressing need for more targeted community provision based on a thorough assessment of individual needs.

## Notes

1. *Report on a Survey of West Indian Pensioners in Nottingham,* Nottinghamshire County Council Social Services Department, 1981.

2. *Elders of the Ethnic Minority Groups,* AFFOR, 1981 and *Black and Asian People in Britain: First Report of a Research Study,* Age Concern Research Unit, 1984.

3. *Triple Jeopardy: Growing old in a second homeland,* Centre for Policy on Ageing, 1985.

# Asian Elders

The 1991 Census results show South Asian (Indian, Pakistani and Bangladeshi) elders over the age of 65 as comprising 2.99% of this age group. However, as with other immigrant communities, these figures do not reflect the concentrated numbers to be found in areas of high settlement.

For those concerned with learning, social and welfare provision for elderly Asians, the issue of diversity within the Asian communities is equally complex. Vaughan Robinson's study of East Africans and South Asians living in Blackburn in 1978 identified as many as 17 distinct minority groups, each with strong individual characteristics related to their rural or urban origins, their degree of adherence to religious and cultural traditions and their relationship to life in Britain. They included rural Indian Gujurati Muslims, urban East African Gujurati Hindus, Pakistani Urdu-speaking Muslims, Punjabi Sikhs and Bengalis. An overview of the Asian communities living in Britain in the 1990s would present an equally complex picture.

Apart from the obvious differences in terms of culture, language, literacy and prior educational experience, it is equally important to distinguish between those elders within the same group who may have arrived in Britain 30 or 40 years ago, in the earlier wave of post-war immigration, and those who came later, as a result of expulsion and political upheaval in the late 70s and early 80s. There are also religious and dietary considerations and differences in attitudes towards women, all of which have important implications not only for the kind of provision offered, but how it is publicised, organised and assessed.

A recent report commissioned by Age Concern, Metro Rochdale and ASHIA (Asian Special Housing Initiative Agency), *Time for Action*, Age Concern Metro Rochdale, 1992, in 1990 outlined a number of findings, based on a series of in-depth interviews with 57 Asian elders, 20 of whom were women. They revealed that:

- 40% of the Asian elders interviewed read or speak English to some extent, and that although a majority are literate in their mother tongue, there is a clear need for non-written forms of communication. The majority of elders experienced difficulty when communicating with statutory agencies

- only 18% of the elders interviewed had access to a car – the majority relied on public transport
- 90% of the elders interviewed were unaware of two out of three selected services provided by the Health Authority, the Local Authority and the voluntary and private sectors
- the majority of elders identified lack of information (84%) and language (72%) as the greatest barriers to receiving assistance
- the mosque played an important social, cultural, religious and educational role within the community and was well attended by elderly men
- 30% of the elders interviewed had contact with libraries and were interested in the mobile library service
- 44% of the elders interviewed expressed a willingness to organise their own social activities with support. Fifty per cent were favourable to integrated (Asian/white) services.

The clearest message emerging from these interviews was the need for information to be communicated in an appropriate language through an accessible medium. Elders repeatedly expressed a demand for more Asian staff to enable direct communication and the delivery of services in a culturally acceptable manner.

# Refugees

Perhaps the most neglected group of black elders are those within the refugee communities, particularly recent arrivals who have spent most of their adult lives in another country and culture. Although their numbers are relatively small and unlikely to be accurately reflected in the most recent Population Survey, their needs are considerable.

A study by Nidia Castro of the Refugee Council revealed three distinct generations of elderly refugees in the London area:

- those from Eastern Europe who arrived before the 1950s such as Armenian, Russian, Jewish, Polish elderly
- those who arrived here in the 1970s and early 1980s mainly from Vietnam, South Africa, Cyprus and countries in Latin America
- those who have arrived since the mid-1980s, including Somalis, Eritreans, Ugandans, Tamils, Iranians, Kurds and, most recently, former Yugoslavians.

The study found that social or educational provision for elderly refugees was most likely to be within communities which have had time to establish themselves. Consequently, there was little evidence of any organised clubs or activities for the small number of elderly refugees in the latter group. This was partly because available resources are still being directed towards the re-settlement of new arrivals of all ages, and partly because their numbers are comparatively small.

In groups that have been here for 10 years or longer, sheltered accommodation, social and luncheon clubs for the elderly and a tradition of voluntary community work is gradually being established, providing not only health and welfare support, but also a number of formal and informal learning activities. These include English language and literacy classes, arts and crafts, cultural and social events, reminiscence work, educational talks, holidays, outings and welfare advice. Talks on health-related issues, fund-raising skills and handling conflict within the family were among the most popular learning activities identified.

# Other Elders

The case studies which follow outline the background and requirements of some of the other ethnic minority elders, including those in the Chinese, Turkish-Cypriot and Latin American communities. They demonstrate clearly that while black elders have much in common in terms of their experience of institutional racism and isolation from mainstream services, they each have a unique set of circumstances which providers can address only if they are prepared to enter into creative partnerships and on-going dialogue with the communities themselves.

# CASE STUDY

# *1*

# Butetown
# History
# &
# Arts Project

**LOCATION:** Butetown ('Tiger Bay'), Cardiff

**TARGET GROUP:** African, Caribbean and Asian elders living in the local community

**AIMS:**

- to ensure that the social history of Butetown (Tiger Bay and the Docks) is carefully collected and preserved for posterity
- to collect and preserve this history with the active involvement of residents and former residents of the Butetown community
- to creatively use visual arts and media arts to produce materials, exhibitions and programmes that are interesting and accessible to a broad audience
- to contribute to multicultural awareness
- to help people from inner-city Cardiff acquire education and training
- to facilitate positive interaction, based on understanding and respect between the old and new communities of Cardiff docklands – through courses, exhibitions, publications and other activities

**OUTCOMES:** Members are given an opportunity to share and relive past life experiences

**PARTNERSHIPS:** Local community with Cardiff Town Development Corporation and Cardiff City Council

**STATUS:** Voluntary

**FUNDING:** Welsh Arts Council, Cardiff Town Development Corporation, Cardiff City Council, British Film Institute, Marks and Spencer, County of South Glamorgan and South East Wales Arts Association

**Butetown History & Arts Project**

The Butetown History and Arts Project is a unique and innovative scheme that has been developed as part of Cardiff's docklands regeneration initiative. Set up by local people, many of them pensioners, it is a collaborative venture involving local elders, professional researchers, artists and media workers.

The five-year project, which began in February 1988, has set out to collect and catalogue over 5,000 old photographs and 3,000 hours of audio-taped oral recollections from Butetown's older residents, including 150 life histories. It will also collect several thousand newspaper articles, old documents and artefacts, and assemble a small library of relevant books, reports and writings. It is intended that these materials will form part of the Bay People's Archive, which will be an invaluable educational and artistic resource for future generations in Butetown and beyond.

The project's work involves extensive contact with Tiger Bay's black elderly population – and its success ultimately depends on their active support, involvement and co-operation.

**Butetown History & Arts Project**

**"/"** Butetown is one of Britain's oldest multi-racial populations and its history goes back nearly 150 years. For a time it was the largest coal exporting port in the world, and black seamen from all over the British empire were drawn here in search of work and out of a curiosity for the Mother Country.

Its reputation was such that if an African seaman happened to mention he was heading for England, he would immediately be advised to go to Tiger Bay, where he could be sure of traditional African hospitality and be made to feel welcome. Our shops catered for every possible culture, and you could get everything from fish and chips to halal meat here.

Older people in the community – and some of them can go back a long, long time – remember Butetown as a vibrant, lively, cosmopolitan place, where the different communities were genuinely integrated. There was a high level of religious tolerance, with Christians and Muslims living and worshipping side by side and their children growing up together. Because the men were at sea a lot of the time, there was a heavy dependence on the Welsh women who, in marrying them, had cast their lot in with the black community, often facing rejection from their own families in the process.

During the war, when black girls from Butetown were bussed in to dances at the local American base so that black GIs, still subject to US segregation laws, could have 'acceptable' dance partners, quite a few liaisons were formed. Some resulted in marriage, and every five years we hold a Butetown Reunion which brings everyone together to visit old friends, reminisce and have a really good time.

So the place has its own unique culture, and because it was such a close-knit, self-reliant community, there is a lot of shared history and experience. People had to learn how to survive on their own resources, and because there was no technology to speak of apart from the radio, this meant learning from each other on a day to day basis about the 'ifs' and 'whys' of life.

The Project began with a meeting in a pub. We began by holding a series of meetings for older people in the community, publicised by word of mouth and the local press, and in the end there were five or six dedicated people who decided to see the project through by applying for funding and premises and getting others involved.

Since it began, the project has run a number of educational courses, ranging from 'Understanding Islam' to 'A History of Blacks in Britain'. Some are aimed specifically at elders in the community; others try to encourage all generations to take part. For example, we organised a lunchtime film and discussion group on 'The Making of Multi-Ethnic Britain', as a way of promoting local people's awareness of the contribution of various immigrant groups to the British/Welsh culture and way of life.

We also ran a course in 'Basic Photography' which encouraged people to bring in their old photographs and learn how to copy them, and invited them to get involved in preparing photo exhibitions on the history of Butetown. That was for everyone, from young people to senior citizens.

Our reminiscence work involves either going out and interviewing the old people in their own homes or inviting them in. Our aim is to get their stories down on film or audio-tape so that we will have a permanent record for future generations. They have given us their old photographs and letters, seamen's discharge papers, passports, immigration cards, ration books and boarding house ledgers. We have also run discussion groups for this purpose, and recently called all the old ex-seamen together. They were able to relive the traumas of being torpedoed during the war and of losing brothers and close friends when the ships went down.

Talking about their lives in this way helps to sharpen their powers of recall and ensures that they can keep the memories alive. It is also very therapeutic because when they relive the past, it adds to their sense of pride and self-worth and encourages them to feel actively involved in the life of the community.

The project has many successes it can point to, but among its most important achievements is the respect it has rekindled among the younger generations. There are still a number of unmet needs among the older population in our community, and there's a lot of isolation still to be overcome. As well as respect, older black people need physical and psychological security, and the confidence of being able to communicate for themselves. These are just some of the many positive side-effects of our project, but they are difficult to measure in educational terms.

# CASE STUDY

# *2*

# The Pepperpot Club

**LOCATION:** Ladbroke Grove, North Kensington

**TARGET GROUP:** African-Caribbean Pensioners

**AIMS:**

- to enhance the quality of life of Club members by providing a setting where they can meet their friends and make new ones; read the books and papers provided; take part in the varied recreational activities; and eat a nutritious balanced midday meal that takes account of dietary needs (e.g. hypertension, diabetes)
- to provide a support service to the elderly members of the local Caribbean community, monitoring their needs and liaising with the statutory services so as to enable them to live independently at home
- to encourage new interests by means of talks, outings and visits to places of interest, including theatres and attending conferences.

**OUTCOMES:**

- members gain companionship, helping to combat loneliness and isolation
- members gain mental stimulation and physical well-being as a result of involvement in educational, recreational and social activities
- members receive advice and support in dealing with statutory agencies
- members receive a hot, nutritious, Caribbean meal every day.

**PARTNERSHIPS:** Originally GLC (Greater London Council); currently funded by the Royal Borough of Kensington and Chelsea with Kensington and Chelsea Adult Education College (craft tutors' part-time hours); and Help the Aged (partial funding of mini-bus)

**STATUS:** Voluntary

**FUNDING:** Royal Borough of Kensington and Chelsea (premises, staff salaries); City Parochial Foundation; Campden Charities (funding for social events); and the Lord Ashton Charitable Settlement (part-time salary).
Supplemented by own fund-raising activities

**The Pepperpot Club**

The African-Caribbean community in 'the Grove', host to the famous Notting Hill Carnival, is one of London's oldest post-war immigrant communities. It has a growing elderly Caribbean population – many of whom settled there in the late forties and early fifties – and a well-established voluntary tradition of catering for the needs of its elderly people.

The Pepperpot Club was established in 1981 when its founder, Pansy Jeffrey, then a worker at the local Citizens Advice Bureau, became increasingly concerned at the number of elderly people she was seeing from the Caribbean who were suffering from loneliness and isolation. The Drop-In Centre for Caribbean elders, which she organised in her office at the CAB in response to this need, was soon to develop into an independent, non-residential day centre.

The Pepperpot Club now has 12 years' experience of catering for African-Caribbean elders in the local community. Its services include a daily luncheon club, a meals-on-wheels service, arts and craft classes, recreational facilities such as dominoes and carpet bowls, keep-fit classes, and regular outings and cultural activities. It has a membership of over 130, and publicises its services through local social services, hospitals and GPs, as well as by word of mouth.

**The Pepperpot Club**

**"/"** The Pepperpot Club is based on the Swinbrooke estate and is a life-line for many of the elderly Caribbean people who live locally. We have seven paid staff and four volunteers, and we cater for people in North Kensington and the vicinity. Those with mobility difficulties are collected each day in our minibus; others make their own way here, including some who come from further afield. Apart from all our activities, we provide a hot Caribbean meal every day, including a meals on wheels service to those who are housebound or can't make it into the centre. There are usually about 35 members in at any one time.

It is true that a lot of our elders would like to have returned home to live out their retirement, but its not that easy for them. Some have been here for 40 or 50 years, and there is no one to go back to. Apart from the uprooting and the loss of friends this would entail, there is also a fear that they would not have access to health care and regular medication. One of our members went home quite recently just to see if he could re-settle, but even though his children are there, he's still undecided about going back.

The Club's members come from all over the Caribbean, although a majority are Jamaicans. There is no evidence of any 'small island' rivalries, and everyone gets on well together. We encourage an atmosphere in which everyone is treated as an equal. A lot of them are very lonely and isolated, and despite the length of time they have been here, they still don't feel part of the society because their needs have been neglected. So the Centre provides them with essential services, and a place to meet that they can call their own.

Ideally, we would like to be able to employ an outreach worker. A lot of the old people are housebound and need someone to come into their homes to read or write letters for them, sort out problems with medication, or just be someone to talk to. Local residential care facilities are very limited, and cater primarily for elderly whites, so there are still a lot of elderly Caribbean people living at home with no support.

Most of our educational activities are arts- and crafts-centred. One of our staff is employed as a tutor to do jewellery-making, soft-toy making, T-shirt decoration and anything else the members decide to try. We also have a part-time tutor supplied by the Kensington and Chelsea Adult Education College who does painting with them and a volunteer who does tapestry. The members raise funds by selling what they make at our annual craft exhibition, when we invite local people, dignitaries and community groups to come and see what we've been doing. This kind of activity helps to slow down the ageing process, and encourages people with eyesight, hearing or loss of memory problems to stay active and alert.

We are also doing on-going reminiscence work. This is organised by the Kensington and Chelsea Community History Group, and resulted two years ago in the publication of a book entitled *Nice Tastin' – Life and Food in the Caribbean.* This is a compilation of poems, recipes, anecdotes and personal accounts of what it was like growing up in the Caribbean. Our members are often invited into local schools to talk to the children about Caribbean food and culture, which is important for the children and a bonus for the old people themselves, who are made to feel that their experience is valued and respected.

There is a lot of informal educational work that goes on here, too. For example, we take them out to the theatre to see black productions and other shows they are interested in which they wouldn't otherwise get to see. We also go on day trips to the seaside or to see the cricket at Lords. Every year we go to a Wine-Tasting Festival in Tunbridge Wells and on a Christmas shopping trip to Calais, and we've recently been on a day-trip to Bruges in Belgium. A lot of our members would not go out alone and are afraid to travel long distances. They feel more secure in a group and they benefit from the chance to discuss where they've been with other members. Plus, it enables us to identify and assist any people with expired passports.

We also have students in on placements, and organise regular talks. People come in to give information and advice on a whole range of things – for example, medical and health matters, managing the household budget and sickle cell anaemia. We had someone from British Telecom in recently to demonstrate some of the equipment that's available for elderly people who are disabled or hearing impaired.

We believe in promoting the achievements of our elderly members as positive role-models in the community, so this year we are organising an Awards Celebration for African-Caribbean elders to raise funds and honour individuals for their contribution to the arts, music, voluntary work, education or business development.

Hopefully this will become an annual event. They receive a small financial award and a certificate. There is also a Pepperpot Award, in recognition of the hard work put in by volunteers and anyone else who has helped with the club's development.

Our greatest difficulties are connected with premises and funding. The Centre is not big enough to cater for all our members, especially when we organise social events like the Christmas party, and it is difficult to organise craft and keep-fit activities in such a cramped space. Ideally we'd like to buy our own premises. We also need more funds so that we can employ more workers and expand the work we're doing.

It's difficult to sum up what the Pepperpot Club has achieved over the past 12 years, but among our most important successes is the role we have played in mediating between elderly members and the statutory services. We are in a position to raise problems on their behalf and to put pressure on them to meet individual needs. What they can tell us, they often can't tell their Social Workers or GPs, who are usually white and may not always be able to recognise the problems. So we have been able to build up a relationship of trust with them and this is vitally important.

We have also given members self-confidence and self-assertion skills. They often come to us claiming that they can't do anything or feeling unable to mix and socialise with others. Having a comfortable, user-friendly space of their own and being able to participate in members' meetings and the Management Committee makes a tremendous difference to how people feel about themselves. I'd have to use the word 'empowerment' here, because that's what it's about.

- concentrate on building trust, respect and a sense of ownership and belonging
- show patience and understanding, and *be seen* to understand by putting your words into action
- make individual members feel important – let them know that you're only here because of them
- involve the members in the organisation's policy and decision-making and maintain a dialogue with them
- keep them informed about everything you do, including financial matters and decisions about the day to day running of the club
- give them control with guidance – control without the necessary support is not enough
- try to be clear about what you're doing and why – and make sure you get the necessary help from the local council and other agencies, so that you can avoid short-term funding arrangements.

GOOD PRACTICE: With African-Caribbean Elders

# CASE
# STUDY

# *3*

Asian
Elderly
Video
Project

**LOCATION:** Southall, West London

**TARGET GROUP:** Asian elderly (Indian, Pakistani, East African)

**AIMS:**

- to extend educational opportunities to elderly people using the centre
- to teach the Asian elderly how to use video equipment
- to encourage communication, discussion and the sharing of life experiences among Centre users
- to link with the Milap oral history project and use video as a way of documenting the experiences of elderly people in the area
- to involve staff at the centre to ensure that the initiative could be continued and developed after the end of the project

**OUTCOMES:**

- members gained new technical skills and an opportunity to share and relive past life experiences
- a video was produced, providing a record for younger members of the community and other interested parties

**PARTNERSHIPS:**

University of London, Centre for Extra-Mural Studies
Milap Day Centre (premises, support staff)
Dominion Community Centre (video equipment)

**STATUS:** Short-term voluntary partnership between Higher Education and non-residential Asian day centre

**FUNDING:** University of London, Centre for Extra-mural Studies (staff training, part-time hours and fees for technical consultancy), Milap Day Centre (premises, support staff), NIACE-REPLAN (staff salaries plus grant for video subtitles)

**Asian Elderly Video Project**

The Asian Elderly Video Project was a short-term initiative based on a partnership between a number of agencies. Based in a non-residential day centre in Southall, it was an innovative example of how to teach elders new skills while at the same time drawing on their wealth of knowledge and experience.

Although the project was completed three years ago, it provides an excellent model of community partnership and co-operation. Careful outreach and needs analysis work in the early stages ensured that the provision was relevant to the needs of those involved. The use of mother-tongue workers and an existing day centre made it possible for the elders to learn in a relaxed, familiar environment in which they felt at home.

The lessons to be learnt from this project are particularly relevant in the current climate of dependence on short-term external funding and co-operative local partnerships.

**Asian Eldeerly Video Project**

The Asian Elderly Video Project was set up after we had done three months of outreach work and visiting local providers. The Milap Day Centre had already attempted some reminiscence work, and the staff were interested in pursuing this. The Centre for Extra-Mural Studies also had an ongoing Media Studies project, and their criteria fitted. So they were able to allocate money for staff training, part-time hours, and technical consultants to assist us with the video work.

The Milap Day Centre was set up in the 1950s to overcome some of the difficulties faced by Asian elders in Southall by providing help with finance, health, housing and family problems. The users are elderly men and women of retirement age and a few younger people who are disabled or unemployed due to long-term illness. They have over 700 registered users taking part in a full programme of lectures, games, film-shows, the Asian meals luncheon club, outings, a regular tea club, craft activities and other educational opportunities. They also do casework and offer welfare advice, a library, a laundry service, an exercise room and the use of their mini-bus for travel assistance.

We met with a group of elders who were already using the Centre and asked them about their interests. We found out when it would suit them to meet, whether they preferred mixed or single-sex provision, and what they would like to do. The idea of learning how to make the video themselves came from them.

The local Creative Media Group and consultants from Real Time, a video collective, helped us with the video-making skills and the actual process involved. The local Dominion Community Centre provided us with the audio-visual equipment, and myself and Vipin, the other Asian worker, came in and taught them the technical skills. But the elders retained control of the project.

We made a contract with the participants which stated that no one was to be videoed without their permission, and that the group was to have control after the making and editing of the video, as well as determine how the completed product was to be used. We agreed that the sessions would be conducted in Punjabi, which was the language most of us had in common. Although it began as a mixed project, it was the women who ended up seeing the project through to completion.

INTERVIEW: Jasbir Panesar (Former Project Worker and Tutor)

Before we could begin, we underwent training. I had never touched video equipment before so I had to learn about the process of making community video from scratch. The course run by Real Time covered how to familiarise the elders with the equipment, and practical games and exercises we could use to teach basic equipment and communication techniques. We also learnt how to make sure they were comfortable and relaxed, and ways of encouraging co-operation and responsibility within the group.

It was also an opportunity to look at issues surrounding racism and sexism, equal opportunities, accountability, editorial control and media representation, all of which equipped us with ideas for the project.

The video project was an opportunity for the elders to learn the use of equipment like cameras, recorders and microphones. We began by encouraging the quietest members of the group to handle the equipment first. We wanted to create a non-competitive environment where everyone could handle equipment at their own pace and be given individual attention. Those who became more confident were encouraged to guide the others.

It was not all plain-sailing, of course. We found that some of the elders had a different sense of time and missed sessions due to forgetfulness or illness. So we had to do a lot of chasing to make sure they attended consistently. Sometimes we needed to go over things again because of forgetfulness. We also had to work hard to maintain their focus in interviews, and their general enthusiasm for the project. They tended not to appreciate the constraints of time and money that govern a short-term project like this.

There were problems with the technical language, too. The commercial names given to the audio-visual equipment were meaningless to them so they were encouraged to think of alternative names that they could relate to. Some also experienced difficulties writing down their ideas for the video. Quite a few of the elders were too frail to carry the heavy camera and recorder so we did this for them. But every effort was made to ensure that they took overall responsibility for the production.

Lack of self-confidence was also an issue. Sometimes, the women were somewhat negative about their own performance and tended to undermine their skills, particularly their interviewing skills and their confidence in handling the equipment.

The members also needed space to get to know one another so that they could work together as a team in what proved to be a very different environment to the one they had been used to.

Despite these problems, the oral history video project was a tremendous learning opportunity for those who took part. From interviewing each other, they gained experience in how to conduct themselves in other formal situations. Social issues like arranged marriage, divorce, and the status of daughters-in-law were popular topics for discussion, and they learnt how to structure their ideas and how to listen to one another. Above all, they learnt to critically analyse the roles they and others play within Asian society, and their perceptions of the younger generation growing up in Britain.

With our guidance, the group eventually produced two videos in Punjabi. One was about the Milap Day Centre, and used interviews with staff and users to highlight the needs of Asian elders in this country. The other, called *Yesterday, Today and Tomorrow*, sets out to document their life experiences, from growing up in East Africa or in the Asian sub-continent prior to partition, to their migration to the UK due to economic circumstances and political upheavals. They have tried to show the importance of living together in tolerance, regardless of religion or caste.

All in all, the project was a unique opportunity to document the lives, struggles and experiences of the Asian elderly in Southall. Their needs, in comparison to other age groups, are virtually ignored within the education system, so there was a strong educational element in it for them from the start. But the project has also enabled some valuable personal history to be recorded, and the videotapes will be a useful community educational resource for others.

- consult with the clients – elders are not incapable of decision-making and should have a full say in how things are run
- make sure the clients have ownership of the project through their involvement in all stages of the project's organisation and delivery
- set yourself realistic time limits – the learning process for older people is inevitably slower and may require more patience
- be aware of clients' other commitments; contrary to the stereotype, not all elders are 'couch cabbages' – they have hospital appointments, babysitting and other things to attend to and your provision needs to be flexible enough to take account of this
- make sure the tutors and project workers speak their language – and can explain technical jargon and cope with the depth of reasoning needed
- make sure they can tune in to the clients' expectations regarding dress and behaviour so that they have credibility and can gain the elders' respect.

**GOOD PRACTICE: With Asian Elders**

# CASE
# STUDY

# *4*

Latin
American
Golden
Years
Project

**LOCATION:** Brixton, South London

**TARGET GROUP:** Chilean and other Latin American refugees (aged 50+)

**AIMS:**

- to help counter the loneliness, depression and isolation of elderly Latin Americans who speak little or no English
- to provide them with a place to meet and a helping hand in their own language
- to provide recreational and leisure activities, advice and counselling, and personal support
- to provide arts and crafts as a form of individual therapy

**OUTCOMES:** Members gain new skills and greater self-confidence

**PARTNERSHIPS:** None, though some advice and support is available from the Refugee Support Centre

**STATUS:** Voluntary

**FUNDING:** Self-financing; small one-off grant from Age Concern

**Latin American Golden Years Project**

The driving force behind the Latin American Golden Years Project is Amada Vergara, herself a Chilean who came to this country with her family as a refugee in the mid-seventies. Amada became increasingly aware of the needs of fellow Chileans when working as a volunteer interpreter in hospitals and it is her entirely voluntary efforts which led to the founding of the group.

The Latin American Golden Years Project was set up by Amada and a group of eight Chilean pensioners in July 1992. Just one year later, the group has grown to 56 from all over London, just over half of whom are women. Although members are not all able to attend the weekly sessions currently based in a community centre in Brixton, Amada makes sure they are kept in touch with the group's activities by means of regular home visits and frequent telephone contact. Their meetings are publicised by word of mouth, and via the mailings of Chile Democratico, an organisation for Chileans in exile.

**Latin American Golden Years Project**

**"/"** In the beginning, we thought we could get together and talk about our country over a cup of tea and an *empanada* (Chilean pie). But we soon realised that it was not to be like that. Everyone knew of someone who was housebound or needing help because they did not speak English. Everyone wanted to learn new skills, in order to earn some pocket money. As one member put it, 'we have dedicated our lives to our husbands and children, and now they are grown up it is our turn to learn something for tomorrow'.

Nearly every member in the group had been in jail or tortured back in Chile. Up until now, they had not been able to talk about these experiences. Others were too ashamed to admit that they had been deserted by their children. As a result, they felt isolated from other Chileans.

We have always thought that we are going back next year, that Britain is not our country. Because of this, we thought we did not need to learn English. But after nearly 20 years in this country, the chances of going back are very slim. I teach English to those who want to learn, just a few words at a time, but mostly they are not motivated to learn in a big group and they feel intimidated at the idea of attending language classes in a College. Because of their state of mind, some also find it difficult to concentrate and remember things. There must be many other elderly Latin Americans in this situation.

I started by teaching them what I knew well – toy-making, dress-making and first-aid. But I soon realised that depressed people want to see fast results. So I went to the library and started to read some therapy books. The first one I picked up was called 'Painting as a Therapy'. Coming home, I decided that if I could teach myself, I could teach others things that could be both a skill and a therapy.

So we started to print leaves from my garden on pieces of fabric. Everyone loved it, and we put together a few things – a cake, a bottle of wine, a soft toy and a bouquet of flowers – and made a raffle which gave us £75. With our monthly membership fees of a pound each, we had £87. We spent all the money on paints, brushes, fabric and a book on stencilling techniques. Ever since then, we have not stopped.

Today, there are between 15 and 20 people attending our regular sessions on Wednesdays. Although you never see the same people every week, apart from about 10 regulars, our membership is over 50. Some attend when they feel like it, and that's fine because I don't think I could cope with everyone at once.

Everything we do is conducted in our language. Sometimes the other members share their knowledge of a particular skill or craft which they learnt when back in Chile. It's not unusual for a new member to need several weeks before they feel able to do more than just sit and watch. But little by little they start to make conversation and become involved in whatever it is we are doing. In this way, their self-confidence slowly returns and they are able to relax and forget their problems for a while.

At the beginning of the year, two good things happened. I was introduced to the Refugee Support Centre, which has helped me a lot by giving advice and support. They also sent along two group therapists to give us demonstrations, one in dance and movement for relaxation purposes, and the other on painting as a form of therapy. They liked this, but no one was ready to continue with it for two reasons. First, although nearly everyone had problems, both past and present, they did not want to discuss them in front of the other members. Secondly, they made it clear that they like what they are already doing, that is the current work of painting on fabrics.

There is a lot of pride and shyness in the group. Everyone has subjective, emotional experiences that they have buried away. What they need is more one-to-one counselling to help them with torture trauma and health matters. One of the therapists is now learning Spanish for this purpose. Although I have been providing this, I have not had any formal training. I think it would be selfish of me to spend the little money we have on a training course. But I find it difficult sometimes, because my experiences are very similar and when I listen to them it stirs up a lot of pain for me.

Our main constraints are money and premises. At present we have the use of one room in a Youth and Community Centre. The place is very busy, and if they have other bookings, we have to cancel our weekly meeting. We would like a more reliable place of our own, somewhere a bit more comfortable where we could store our materials. Travel is also a problem. At the moment I do home visits on my motor-bike. It is also difficult for some members to make the journey here on public transport.

Unfortunately, we don't have enough money to give a full service and incorporate things like jewellery-making, which would help those who suffer from arthritis in their hands, and other crafts like toy-making. We'd like to be able to sell things at Christmas and perhaps raise enough money to buy a second-hand van so that we could go on outings. Up until now, we have looked at England and compared it with Latin America, and we have not enjoyed what we have seen. This way we could see this country in a different way.

- start small – it can take a year to work out the funding and resources that the group needs
- be realistic about what you can achieve – and take it one step at a time
- don't impose your own views – be prepared to learn from the clients themselves and observe their needs first hand
- don't try to cut yourself into pieces – volunteers should seek professional help where it is available
- develop informal responses – ones that allow people to move at their own pace and which don't frighten them away
- make links with other agencies that can offer support and expertise; where they don't exist, make sure that other voluntary organisations and local authority services know that they are needed
- ask for health and welfare leaflets and other information to be translated into the relevant languages – the language barrier is probably the greatest cause of isolation
- use mother tongue for classes and discussions, and where necessary offer individuals help with translation and interpreting
- keep less active members informed and involved by making home visits and regular phone-calls
- encourage members to bring their friends and families along to learn and contribute whatever they can.

**GOOD PRACTICE: With Elderly Refugees**

# CASE
# STUDY

# 5

Turkish-
Cypriot
Elders
Project

**Turkish-Cypriot Elders Project**

**LOCATION:** Haringey, North London

**TARGET GROUP:** Turkish-Cypriot pensioners living in the local community

**AIMS:**

- to provide a mobile welfare rights service to Turkish-speaking pensioners in Haringey with a special emphasis on those who are housebound either because of a disability or because of cultural or language barriers
- to improve clients' knowledge and awareness of available services and help them to overcome their anxieties about accessing them
- to provide suitable translated literature
- to provide an opportunity to learn English to enable clients to take advantage of mainstream services
- to provide a weekly luncheon club and a regular meeting place, offering culturally appropriate food and activities.

**OUTCOMES:** Clients receive information, advice and welfare support; and the stimulation of communicating with others with whom they share a common language and cultural background

**PARTNERSHIPS:** Age Concern, Haringey Council, Turkish-Cypriot Youth Association

**STATUS:** Voluntary

**FUNDING:** Home Office (Section 11); London Borough of Haringey; Age Concern

**Turkish-Cypriot Elders Project**

Haringey is home to a large Cypriot community of both Greek and Turkish origin. Age Concern workers became aware of the need for targeted provision when monitoring take-up of its regular services to local pensioners.

It was clear that Turkish-Cypriot elders were among a number of ethnic minority groups who were isolated from mainstream provision and not gaining access to available services. On this basis, they were able to make a successful application for Section 11 funding for a three-year Turkish-Cypriot Elders Project with the support of the local council, which pays the two seconded workers' salaries.

The main reason for the isolation of Turkish-Cypriot elders is the language barrier, compounded by religious differences (99% are Muslims). Because they live in a relatively well-established community with its own shops, banks, cafés and other facilities, many elderly Turkish-Cypriots have had little prior exposure to life and services in the wider community.

The project employs two mother-tongue workers and has made active contact with about 100 pensioners, around 30 of whom meet weekly in a room supplied by the local Turkish-Cypriot Youth Association for a variety of activities. The group is advertised by word of mouth, and through the local Turkish-Cypriot newspapers *Toplum Postasi* and *Pazar* which are freely available in local libraries, delicatessens and selected news-stands.

**" / "** My role is to make contact with Turkish-Cypriot pensioners, particularly those who are in need of care, and to make sure they get the information and support they should be getting. I do this mainly by making home visits, and by encouraging those who can to come along to our weekly Turkish-Cypriot Elders club where they can eat Turkish food, watch Turkish films, listen to Turkish music, play cards or bingo together and say prayers for lost relatives. Sometimes they are happy to just sit and talk and to benefit from having a chance to communicate with others in their own language.

As in other communities, there were several waves of Cypriot immigrants. The first group came to this country in the fifties and sixties, mainly as young men seeking work and education. Until quite recently there was no Higher Education to speak of in Cyprus, so because of the colonial ties with Britain, this was an obvious choice for those who, for whatever reason, did not prefer to go to Turkey. Most brought their families with them or sent for them as soon as they had settled. Probably about 60% of those who attend our project belong to this group.

The second wave came in 1974, when events in Cyprus led to a mass exodus of both Greek- and Turkish-Cypriots. They were fleeing the violence and the uncertainty of their futures in the aftermath of the hostilities which led to the island's partition. There was a huge population upheaval at this time, as well as loss of life, homes and farming lands.

The third group consists of the grandparents of those who came earlier, those whose children sent for them when they became too old to care for themselves. They are in the minority and have mostly arrived since the mid-eighties.

The Turkish-Cypriot population is still relatively young even though we now have third and fourth generations growing up here. But the community is becoming more mobile, and as younger people move away, families are becoming dispersed. It is a myth that our elderly can rely on the extended family. Family members may be living close by but they do not necessarily live under the same roof, so there are growing numbers approaching retirement age whose needs will have to be catered for.

**INTERVIEW: Chetin Ahmet (Project Worker)**

The main problem for the elderly in our community is the language barrier, which is actually a disability. Many Turkish-Cypriot elders are not literate in their first language, so although there are some leaflets translated into Turkish, these are of no use to them unless they can depend on a son or daughter to read to them.

It is not uncommon to find second and third generation children who are no longer able to communicate properly with their parents because the parents speak no English and they themselves have gradually forgotten how to speak either Turkish or Greek since they have no use for it outside the home. This is why we are currently planning language classes, to teach basic English to those elders who for the first time find themselves needing to communicate in English and function outside the home.

Haringey is one of the better boroughs in terms of catering for ethnic minority needs, but there are still huge gaps in provision. For example, a lot of local agencies do not employ bilingual workers, so Turkish-Cypriot elders are largely ignorant of welfare benefits and other entitlements. It's not just a language issue, though. Agencies need to employ people who understand the culture and society in which these elders have grown up.

For example, there is no comparable system of welfare support in Cyprus, so elderly Cypriots have no real concept of how the system works here. Most of them still remember the appalling conditions in the Poor Houses in Cyprus, and they are often resistant to the idea of sheltered or residential homes for fear that they are going to be like that. There is also a high incidence of diabetes among Turkish-Cypriot elders, and health-related problems related to fasting during Ramadan.

So our project plays a very important two-way educational role, communicating essential information verbally, on a one-to-one basis, or with the help of translated leaflets and group advice sessions; and mediating between our clients and other local agencies.

Thanks to the support of Age Concern workers, the Turkish Youth Association, community nurses and others, we are able to run group sessions either in Turkish or with the aid of translators, to raise awareness of what is available in terms of social security, housing and voluntary support, and to promote better dietary and primary health care awareness. We find that our pensioners are most comfortable learning in a situation where they are actually able to see or experience the service on offer, so wherever possible we arrange transport and take them out on visits.

We are also busy organising a cultural day, when Turkish-Cypriot youth will be performing folk dances and music. We find this kind of activity helps to promote much-needed communication between the different generations.

Sometimes there are problems we can't deal with because we are not trained counsellors, but fortunately there is a Turkish-Cypriot Women's Project which can offer this kind of support. I don't want to set up a stereotype, because it is not true in every case, but it is fair to say that older women in our community tend to have been confined to the home, caring for children or doing machine work for the rag-trade. Some have very little family support now and are reluctant to venture outside the home.

There is less out there in terms of support for the men, but they at least have the advantage of social cafés where they can gather together to watch Turkish programmes on satellite TV, play cards or just gossip. The women do not have the same kind of social outlet and they are usually more isolated.

So our project offers a variety of social and informal educational activities, and it is the elders themselves who decide on the agenda. This is probably the most important feature of any project like ours – that we have tried to get the elders actively involved from day one. Bureaucrats tend to make assumptions which are based on stereotypes and ignorance of the culture and they forget to ask the clients what *they* want.

Another very important feature is the employment of mother-tongue workers like myself and my co-worker, because we have a good knowledge of the community and culture, and can convey jargon and unfamiliar concepts in a language the elders can understand. We can also communicate with their carers, often daughters or daughters-in-law, who are burdened with the task of caring for elderly relatives. They are isolated too, and they mostly suffer in silence.

It is hard to separate out the educational benefits from the social and other benefits they receive. But there is no doubt that Turkish-Cypriot elders learn a great deal from their involvement in our project; and that the mental stimulation they get from taking part in group activities, discussions and outings helps to keep them active, involved and mentally alert into their old age.

# CASE
# STUDY

# *6*

## Chinese
## Elders
## Club

**LOCATION:** Newcastle-upon-Tyne

**TARGET GROUPS:** Chinese Elders (aged 50+)

**AIMS**:

- to provide a regular lunch, social activities and a meeting place for Chinese elders in the local community
- to provide them with an opportunity to talk and meet together

**OUTCOMES:**

- members gain up-to-date information on benefits, housing needs, etc. leading to greater independence
- frail and housebound users are less isolated
- trust is developed, leading to take up of other Age Concern services, including carer and day-care support

**PARTNERSHIPS:** Age Concern with North-East Chinese Association and Newcastle City Council Community Services

**STATUS:** Voluntary

**FUNDING:** Age Concern, Newcastle, with occasional income from members' fund-raising activities

**Chinese Elders Club**

There are small but visible Chinese communities in almost every major British city, many of which were established over a hundred years ago. In Newcastle's case, the community has grown up since 1943, when one of their current elders established a restaurant and subsequently a factory supplying specialist sauces and foodstuffs to Chinese caterers in the region. Others followed, usually with the expectation of finding work there.

Fifty years on, Newcastle's Chinese community officially stands at 1213, and includes a small but significant number of elderly people. Although identified in the latest Census as comprising only 43, the number of over-65s is unofficially estimated to be considerably higher, possibly as many as 120.

Age Concern was keenly aware of the lack of take-up of their services by this group for some time, but it was discussions initiated by the North-East Chinese Association in 1990 which led to the need being formally recognised and the development of targeted provision.

The weekly club offers a warm, welcoming venue where Chinese elders can meet, eat authentic food supplied by a local Chinese restaurant and engage in a number of formal and informal learning activities, including a weekly English language class. The club is well-attended by over 50 members, and is well-supported by younger members of the community as well as local restaurateurs. It is publicised by word of mouth and through the mailings of the North East Chinese Association and the local Racial Equality Council.

**Chinese Elders Club**

**"** I suppose Age Concern act as enablers. We work closely with the North-East Chinese Association to organise an on-going exchange of up-to-date information and our aim is to help Chinese elders to be as independent as possible by ensuring that each individual receives the support he or she needs.

The Chinese Club is based at the local Chinese community centre, and it is always a hive of activity. The majority of members are Chinese, although there are also quite a number of Vietnamese elders who attend. They haven't got the facilities to cook a full meal on the premises, the kitchen is too small, but the elders do cook their own rice and a local restaurant provides the meat and vegetable dishes at a very reasonable rate. Newcastle's Meals on Wheels service does not provide ethnic Chinese food so for those who can no longer cook for themselves, this is the one time each week when they can eat their own food.

We also arrange regular medical check-ups – health issues tend to be a big thing among Chinese elders, although they tend to prefer a mixture of traditional Chinese and Western medicine. We are fortunate to have a qualified Chinese GP and Health Visitor, and one or other of them attends the club on a regular monthly basis to take blood pressure, monitor weight and give general health check-ups.

There are regular outings to places of interest, and talks and advice sessions, because we have found that because of language barriers, elderly Chinese people are generally poorly informed about their welfare, housing and benefits entitlements. Health topics and hairdressing are also very popular – we recently had a hairdresser come in to give them a demonstration, because some members of the group like to cut each others' hair.

There are some needs we are unable to meet, of course. The elders would benefit from a basic maths class, and a mobile library catering for those who can only read books in Chinese. There is a real need for a local Chinese chemist to handle their prescriptions; and for more sheltered housing specifically for Chinese pensioners. We are hoping that a complex of sheltered flats for Chinese elders that is currently being built will be ready for occupation next year. In fact, discussions about this housing project and how it can meet the needs of the elders have really brought the community together.

The weekly English language class attracts between 10 and 15 regular attenders. We originally approached ALBSU (Adult Literacy and Basic Skills Unit) for assistance, but the tutor's part-time hours are currently paid for by the local adult education service.

The Chinese Club has been going for three years now. It hasn't always been smooth-sailing, particularly in the early days. There was some factionalism within the Chinese community that had to be resolved, and we also had to work hard to earn their trust. We have achieved this by means of constant communication with the community's elders and spokespeople – we regularly meet together to discuss issues over a Chinese meal.

We also make sure that members are kept informed about everything we do – for example, we post information up on the noticeboard giving a detailed account of how their monies are used. We attempt to meet any requests as they arise, and the group is constantly being encouraged to take an active part in determining activities from one month to the next.

For the past six years, Age Concern has also been running a Vietnamese club in partnership with the Ockenden Venture. This meets monthly, and offers a similar informal advice service and social and luncheon club. Unfortunately, our attempts to introduce formal activities apart from games have not met with the same success, possibly because they meet less often. Even so, the membership is fairly consistent and Vietnamese elders gain a lot in terms of friendship and support.

# CASE STUDY

# 7

## Leicester - Focus on a City

Leicester, with an estimated elderly black population of 26%, provides an appropriate focus for a case study of city-wide educational provision for older black adults. Through its network of statutory and voluntary providers, it has developed a comprehensive range of learning opportunities, many of which cater directly to the needs of its elderly black residents.

Although recent changes in funding mean that there is no longer a statutory obligation to provide non-vocational adult education – traditionally the kind of courses which have attracted older adults – providers of adult and continuing education in Leicester have continued to adhere to a notion of community entitlement to life-long learning.

The following extract from the *Induction and Support Pack for Part-time Tutors of Adults*, Leicestershire Adult Education Service, outlines the context in which adult and continuing education is delivered, and summarises the philosophy which has, until now, underpinned Leicestershire's community education policy.

**LEICESTER: Focus on a City**

*The research and interviews for this section were conducted by Jenny Martin*

# ADULT AND CONTINUING EDUCATION

## What it is and why we have it

Once upon a time - all good induction packs should begin thus - communities looked after their own learning needs. Parents coached their children in the skills needed for paid work or domestic crafts. Recreational skills were developed by networks in the rural or urban village. Culture was celebrated and handed down from generation to generation. Social support came through the extended family.

In the 1990s, the pace of social and economic change is dramatic and brings with it substantial learning needs - at a time when urbanisation, industrialisation and the new communications have undermined the informal learning and support structures previously found in local communities.

Adults need access to learning opportunities for a number of reasons:

**Physical** for both recreational and health purposes.

**Creative Arts** for self-expression and fulfilment in an increasingly passive society.

**Practical Skills** including cookery, DIY, budgeting, domestic craft-skills for survival as well as recreation.

**Personal Development** including assertiveness, coping with stress, the self-esteem that comes with achievement in whatever sphere.

**Life Changes** - learning to cope creatively with parenting, redundancy, pre-retirement, bereavement, returning to work.

**Essential Adult Education** - the development of literacy, numeracy, language and study skills.

**Cultural Identity** - including black studies, community languages, rural crafts, folk music from all cultures.

**Retraining** - the relative shortage of 16-19 year olds in the economy in the 1990s and the overall skills gap between ourselves and our economic competitors highlights the need for increased numbers of skilled adults.

**Career Development** chances to reflect on current skills and achievement with educational guidance and to take steps towards gaining qualifications needed.

Two additional strands run through all adult learning:

**Combating Isolation**. Research shows that over 50% of learners are looking for a positive social experience as much as subject learning.

**The importance of developing our skills as learners**. Factual information nowadays - and even concepts - are often soon outdated and we need to develop independent updating skills. We, too, are increasingly faced with new experiences in everyday living to which we have to find our own solutions.

**All this makes for a major role that Adult and Continuing Education can play in individual, economic and community development.**

71

## The Leicestershire Context

**Leicestershire believes that adults have an entitlement to education.**

In Leicestershire, educational opportunities for adults are provided through **a variety of institutions and organisations.**

- 37 Community Colleges
- 30 Community Centres based on Primary Schools
- 3 Community Centres based on High Schools
- 10 Evening Centres
- 8 Youth and Community Centres or Community Education Projects
- 7 Colleges of Further Education
- 1 College of Adult Education
- 1 Agricultural College
- The Workers' Educational Association
- Leicester University
- De Montfort University
- A variety of other agencies, mostly voluntary organisations like the Councils for Voluntary Services, but also statutory ones like the Health Education Department
- Substantial further provision is organised through the Adult Basic Education Service and the 'English for Speakers of Other Languages Scheme'.
- In addition a number of schools and other premises are used as annexes or 'out-centres' by Community Education establishments.

**Adult Learning Opportunities:**
- Over 4,200 adult education courses were offered in 1991-92.
- Nearly 44,000 people are enroled into courses.
- Some 12% of the courses offer accreditation.
- Over 80% of the courses are self-financing in terms of course fees and tutor costs.

In the management of Adult Learning programmes Leicestershire has a tradition of commitment to local participation and control in shaping the provision at colleges, centres and projects. In the past this has meant that the responsibility has been devolved to local Councils or Management Committees at local level. Within the new Scheme of Management designed to meet the requirements of Local Governance of Schools and new legislation regarding local financial management there is much concern and commitment to continue to involve local people in the design and delivery of Adult Learning programmes. Whilst it has become essential to involve Governing Bodies in the management of Community Education, it has also become evident that the participation by the community has continued to be valued. Many Governing Bodies are seeking ways of encouraging that involvement and developing arrangements that clearly endorse the participation of the adult community.

**The Education of Adults has an important part to play in the development of Leicestershire's Schools, Colleges and Centres.**

from *Induction and Support Pack for Part-time Tutors of Adults*, Leicestershire Adult Education Service

It is within this context of community participation and local delivery that a number courses, services and activities are offered which are of particular interest or relevance to older black people. These include:

- ESOL (English for Speakers of Other Languages)
- Reminiscence work
- Newspaper reading and discussion groups (male)
- Asian and general clothing craft course (women only)
- Information technology
- Craft skills
- Elderly clubs
- Luncheon clubs
- Visiting speakers
- Outings for targeted groups
- Society meetings
- Leisure activities
- Yoga/keep fit
- Swimming for women and girls
- Video club
- Card club
- Visits by the mobile library
- Translation and interpreting services
- Referrals to specialist agencies (e.g. Society for the Blind)

For the purposes of this study, a number of centres serving the needs of black elders in Leicester were selected and both staff and clients were interviewed. As in the previous case studies, standard questions were used (see Appendix 3). Among those visited were four statutory adult education centres, four voluntary projects and a church project.

The aim of these interviews was to identify the diversity of learning needs within the black (predominantly Asian) elderly population and to establish how the different agencies have responded to them. Although each individual project was able to point to unmet needs, and to constraints which have inhibited consistent good practice, they nevertheless provide a useful insight into the different ways communities are responding to the needs of elderly Asian people.

**TARGET GROUP:** Local elders resident in the community

**AIMS:** To provide local residents with community and adult education, youth work and community development opportunities

**OUTCOMES:** Members have a place to meet and share experiences; group activities provide stimulation and help to combat loneliness and isolation

**PARTNERSHIPS:** Age Concern

**STATUS:** Youth and Community Centre

**FUNDING:** Local Education Authority

**PUBLICITY:** Brochure, with additional publicity through Age Concern

**AVALON COMMUNITY EDUCATION PROJECT: Asian Elders Group**

The Avalon Community Education Project runs two groups for elderly local people, one exclusively for Asian elders, each offering informal group activities devised by the clients themselves. The need for this provision was identified by means of a community profile of the local neighbourhood, which revealed that over a quarter of local residents are elderly. A variety of activities are on offer including:

- calligraphy
- tie-dyeing
- flower-making
- flower-arranging
- table-tennis
- lacemaking
- silk-dyeing
- modelling
- knitting.

Even some elders who find work with the hands difficult, due to arthritis, choose to come into the project for the company and stimulation. They claim that their involvement makes them feel useful and needed – a view shared by their tutor, who pointed to the wealth of experience which the centre has been able to tap.

Avalon's other community education classes, catering for all ages and ethnic groups, succeed in attracting 30–40% of their clients from the older (50+) age-group. These are run on a roll-on, roll-off basis.

## CONSTRAINTS/UNMET NEEDS

- The difficulties of trying to establish a common language and develop a shared understanding of what we mean by 'a stimulating education programme for elderly Asians'.

- Constant awareness of the vulnerability of the project due to threatened loss of funding, leading to a general sense of frustration, anxiety and insecurity.

## BEST FEATURES/SUCCESSES

- Ability to offer a 65% fee remission to all OAPs in the area.
- Active targeting of local elderly people, who make up a quarter of the local population.

**AVALON COMMUNITY EDUCATION PROJECT: Asian Elders Group**

- Active participation of elders in the campaign to defend their provision when threatened with closure, including a letter-writing campaign and lobbying of local councillors. This resulted in a reprieve, and the job of their multi-talented tutor was saved.

**AVALON COMMUNITY EDUCATION PROJECT: Asian Elders Group**

**TARGET GROUP:** Members of the local Chinese, Philippino and Malaysian community

**AIMS:** To provide members of the local Chinese, Philippino and Malaysian community with social, educational, jobsearch and welfare support

**OUTCOMES:**

- members with a shared experience have a place to meet
- individuals receive help and advice with personal, employment and language difficulties
- group activities and outings provide stimulation and help to combat isolation and depression

**PARTNERSHIPS:** Local Education Authority

**STATUS:** Voluntary

**FUNDING:** Leicester City Council and Leicester County Council and voluntary contributions

**PUBLICITY:** Bi-lingual (Chinese/English) newsletter/word of mouth

LEICESTERSHIRE CHINESE COMMUNITY CENTRE

The Leicester Chinese Community Centre provides a targeted service designed to meet the needs of the local Chinese population.

The activities on offer include:

- Chinese language classes
- English language classes
- Youth club
- Welfare benefits advice
- Luncheon club for the elderly
- Philippines society
- Employment club
- Tai Chi club
- Malaysian society

For Chinese elders, the Centre provides a weekly meeting place offering Chinese food, informal activities, cultural activities, outings and a venue for birthday parties. Open six days a week on a drop-in basis – some are keyholders and attend every day. Members have access to Chinese videos and games, a library and a kitchen. They also receive assistance, if requested, with official letters and visits to outside agencies, when help with translation or interpreting may be needed.

The Centre relies heavily on volunteers and on the commitment of its staff, who recognise the need for its work to expand.

## CONSTRAINTS/UNMET NEEDS

- Lack of reminiscence work and documentation to highlight the history of Chinese people in Leicester and gather resources for a Chinese Museum.
- Lack of knowledge of available facilities for the elderly – for example, when organising visits to places outside Leicester.
- Currently organising classes for the elderly on how British society works – for example, the benefits system. Conducted in Chinese, these will run after the weekly Luncheon club which meets each Thursday.

## BEST FEATURES/SUCCESSES

- The quality of members' lives is improved and the workers are able to make the members' lives much happier.

**LEICESTERSHIRE CHINESE COMMUNITY CENTRE**

- Use of newsletter to keep membership informed and involved.
- Members are encouraged to take part in a variety of activities including those in the wider community.
- Staff are flexible and prepared to make changes on the basis of feedback received.
- Good liaison and communication with the Management Committee facilitates the smooth running of the Centre.

**LEICESTERSHIRE CHINESE COMMUNITY CENTRE**

**TARGET GROUP:** Members of the local Vietnamese community

**AIMS:**

- to provide members of the local Vietnamese community with support for employment and small business enterprise

- to provide advice and help with general problems

**OUTCOMES:** Individuals receive help and advice with personal, employment and language difficulties

**PARTNERSHIPS:** Leicester Social Services

**STATUS:** Voluntary

**FUNDING:** Local TEC, Department of the Environment, Leicester City and Leicester County Councils, Telethon Trust

**PUBLICITY:** Letters and leaflets sent to Vietnamese families in the local community

**LEICESTER VIETNAMESE ASSOCIATION: Employment, Training & Advice Centre**

The Employment and Training Centre for Vietnamese people was set up in 1986 in response to the needs of a small but growing local Vietnamese community. The Centre provides advice to local people on employment and business matters, and offers English language classes and a fortnightly luncheon club to Vietnamese elders.

For the first two years, the Centre relied on volunteers and received no funding. However, after applying to the local TEC and with the assistance of the two local councils, it is now able to employ three paid workers, and to subsidise meals by £1.45 per head. Staff work in partnership with Social Services, giving support and advice on a range of issues, and where necessary referring clients to other specialist agencies.

## CONSTRAINTS/UNMET NEEDS

- Lack of funding to subsidise outings.
- Inadequate premises, particularly the lack of a kitchen and large hall for social functions.
- Need for more volunteers – for example, to collect old people from their homes.
- Lack of sufficient funding to offer a comprehensive service.

## BEST FEATURES/SUCCESSES

- The quality of members' lives is improved.
- The opportunity to socialise with other Vietnamese makes the elders' lives much happier.

**LEICESTER VIETNAMESE ASSOCIATION: Employment, Training & Advice Centre**

**TARGET GROUP:** Elderly Asian women living in the local community

**AIMS:** To provide English language and related courses, both centre-based and in the form of home tuition

**OUTCOMES:**

- Improved English language communication skills leading to increased confidence and independence
- Elders are able to communicate better and are therefore less isolated

**PARTNERSHIPS:** Age Concern

**STATUS:** Adult Education

**FUNDING:** Home Office (Section 11), FEFC (Further Education Funding Council)

**PUBLICITY:** Community (mother-tongue) radio, via own Newsletter and other community groups and voluntary organisations and by word of mouth

**BELGRAVE BAHENO: English Language Scheme**

Belgrave Baheno is a long-standing community project which works actively to address the needs of local women, particularly those of Asian women and girls. Set up in 1979, it offers computing, book-keeping and childcare courses; counselling and referrals; and provides meeting space, a library, a crèche/after-school playscheme, an exercise room and a sauna. Educational and cultural activities are given a high profile, as are social and recreational events which attract family members of all ages.

Adult education courses at the Centre attract members of all ages, including pensioners. Some are offered as 'tasters' or 'one-off' classes, giving members an opportunity to participate in something new. They include:

- cookery
- keep-fit
- Indian classical singing
- Gujarati
- self-defence
- English for beginners
- batik
- saree painting
- acupuncture/skin-care
- book-keeping
- aromatherapy.

The English language class, which is the only targeted provision for elders, has now been running for several years and resulted from an approach by Age Concern. As well as providing a course at the centre, volunteers offer home tuition in small groups or on a one-to-one basis. Age Concern continues to support the project by arranging transport and a local pick-up service.

## CONSTRAINTS/UNMET NEEDS:
- Despite the need for more of such provision, current funding does not allow for any expansion.
- Transport problems can disrupt timing of classes.
- Current venue has restricted space and is unable to provide wheelchair access to upper floors.

**BELGRAVE BAHENO: English Language Scheme**

## BEST FEATURES/SUCCESSES:

- Ability to cater for those who are housebound or mobility-impaired by providing transport and tuition in the home.
- Regular feedback and evaluation from the users' group and local consultation meetings.
- Elders gain considerable confidence, have an opportunity to meet others and are better able to communicate with grandchildren, GPs, house calls, telephone enquirers, etc.

**BELGRAVE BAHENO: English Language Scheme**

**TARGET GROUP:** Elderly Asians living in the neighbourhood

**AIMS:**

- to befriend elderly people with language problems who are living in the local neighbourhood
- to encourage them to join the group and participate in the running of social and cultural activities

**OUTCOMES**: 'Each individual learns from the group and the group learns something from each individual'

**PARTNERSHIPS:** None

**STATUS:** Voluntary

**FUNDING:** None, except caretaking expenses covered by the Urban Policies Sub-committee

**PUBLICITY:** By leaflet and word of mouth

**WESLEY HALL COMMUNITY PROJECT: Old People's Society**

The Wesley Hall Community Project is a lively, church-based community resource. It offers support to a number of local groups, including young people, parents and those with mental health problems.

Activities based at the project include:

- the Navjivan Lunch Club, sponsored by Age Concern
- the Sahara Scheme, supporting Asian carers of mentally frail relatives
- the Vikram Youth club, catering for Asian young people
- the Mental Health Day Centre, for those suffering or recovering from a mental health problem
- breakfast scheme offering meals to homeless people
- parentcraft, offering advice and childcare videos with the help of an interpreter
- crèche and playgroup for pre-school children
- city councillors' surgery
- coffee bar.

The Old People's Society is a self-supported group and provides a daily meeting space at the Project for elderly Asians, who come together to play cards, make tea, discuss matters of mutual interest and celebrate festive occasions. The group also arranges talks by visiting speakers on topics such as health, welfare benefits, immigration and pensioners' rights.

Responding to a need that was identified by existing project members, the club is self-supporting and receives no outside funding.

## CONSTRAINTS/UNMET NEEDS

- Apathy and lack of motivation on the part of some elders, who may need to be persuaded to depart from the usual daily routine.
- Inability to reach elders who are housebound, whose needs therefore remain unmet.

**WESLEY HALL COMMUNITY PROJECT: Old People's Society**

## BEST FEATURES/SUCCESSES

- The group's self-reliance.

- The project caters for all ages and different groups in the community and provides Asian elders with an opportunity to meet and interact with others.

**WESLEY HALL COMMUNITY PROJECT: Old People's Society**

**TARGET GROUP:** Local adults

**AIMS:** To facilitate access into education in the broadest sense for adults who are unwaged or unemployed, and those who may have had poor educational experiences or been away from education for a long time

**OUTCOMES:** Individuals have an opportunity to share and learn new skills in a very varied group in terms of age, culture and ethnicity, and in a relaxed, friendly, supportive environment

**PARTNERSHIPS:** Originally set up in 1975 in partnership with five other centres as part of the Inner Area Programme

**STATUS:** Adult Education (previously run for seven years as an independent project within the College's Community Education Department)

**FUNDING:** LEA Main Programme, Unwaged Adults Fund

**PUBLICITY:** Outreach – door-to-door leafleting; poster and leaflets in local shops, community centres, launderettes, churches, etc.

**WESTCOTES OPEN WORKSHOPS: Leicester South Fields College**

The Westcotes Open Workshops at Leicester South Fields College organise no specially targeted provision for elders. They are open to people of all ages, and provide a relaxed, supportive learning environment. Because of the flexibility of open learning, and the opportunity to do 'tasters' and other courses on a roll-on, roll-off basis, Asian elders are attracted in significant numbers.

The need for open learning was identified by the College through its guidance activities and anonymous questionnaires. Existing users were also consulted. A number of one-term taster workshops were organised, leading to the establishment of those which have proved most popular. For Asian elders, these include:

- Asian and general clothing crafts
- basic skills (English and Maths)
- photography (women only)
- information technology

The Asian and General Clothing Crafts workshop is particularly popular with elderly Asian women, possibly because it is an area in which they already have skills. They therefore feel more confident about coming into the College.

## CONSTRAINTS/UNMET NEEDS:

- Lack of space for social contact (students are integrated into mainstream college courses and have no base of their own).
- Financial constraints and conditions of funding which limit development of further provision (e.g. more flexi-learning, taster courses, etc.).
- Funding bodies' lack of appreciation of users needs – e.g. the lack of lifts, the one-year attendance limit for most adult learners, etc.
- Lack of disabled access.

## BEST FEATURES/SUCCESSES

- The diversity of students (currently aged 19 to 65, from five different ethnic groups).
- The involvement of users in decision-making, which gives them a 'stake' in the workshops.
- Ongoing educational guidance – the guidance workers see everyone before they start, and they maintain contact on a weekly

WESTCOTES OPEN WORKSHOPS: Leicester South Fields College

basis, so users know they are interested in their individual needs, progress and eventual progression.

- access to **free** quality tutoring in small groups of 6–10 with equipment and learning resources provided.

**WESTCOTES OPEN WORKSHOPS:** Leicester South Fields College

Three older African-Caribbean women living in Leicester were interviewed and asked to describe their past and current experiences of education. One is approaching retirement and has only recently become involved in adult education; one has had to retire early due to ill-health, but has a long history of attending evening classes, which she continues to do; and the other has been a pensioner for some years, and has been able to take advantage of a number of adult learning opportunities.

Although they are not necessarily typical in terms of their prior educational achievement or their experiences of adult learning in this country, they nevertheless have much in common both with each other and with a growing number of their peers. All three have been in this country for over 30 years, and have worked hard to raise and educate their children for much of this time. All have recent or current experiences of mainstream adult education classes, which they attend alongside people of all ages and from a number of other ethnic groups. And all of them are actively involved in their local church, which provides them with an important social and educational stimulus.

Among the most noteworthy aspects of their common learning experience is that each of them sees education as a lifelong process, in which they intend to continue to participate, regardless of age or infirmity.

**AFRICAN-CARIBBEAN ELDERS IN LEICESTER: Individual Case Studies**

**CASE STUDY 1:** Mrs C.

**AGE:** 58

**STATUS:** Early retirement due to ill health

**NO. OF CHILDREN:** Seven

**YEARS IN THE UK:** 32

**COUNTRY OF BIRTH:** Antigua

Since Mrs C. discovered adult education classes over twenty years ago, she has made it her duty to share her knowledge and information with others. She regarded her interview for this project in this context, and was pleased to share her experiences.

She describes her education up to her teenage years as 'good'. She had 12 years of schooling in Antigua, and at that time had wanted to become a teacher. When she married at 18, it was no longer possible to pursue the idea of teacher training. On reflection, she does not think she would have enjoyed teaching. She would probably have ended up teaching theoretical subjects, whereas she finds that working creatively with her hands has brought her much enjoyment in life.

Mrs C. is the mother of seven children. She came to England in 1961 both to join her sister and to 'improve herself'. Unfortunately she was widowed when all the children were still of school-age. She did not remarry, but worked as a nursing auxiliary to support them.

She has had a vicarious life through her children and at no stage did any of them ever bring her a bad school report. However, education had always been dear to her and she felt that if she went to evening classes to learn new skills, she would be better able to help them and to understand their experience as students. This expectation has been realised, as each one of her children has gained from her experience of adult education.

For example, her crowning glory some years ago was when one of her daughters, who is a professional model in London, modelled some of Mrs C.'s creations made on the Multi-Cultural Fashion Course she was attending. Because of the success of her children, she feels gratified as a mother – particularly since she has had very little help. Her own mother did not arrive here until two years ago and she has had no family network to support her. She puts part of her success as a mother to the widening of her horizons and meeting other people which attendance at adult education classes made possible for her.

Not long after coming to England, she obtained employment as a nursing auxiliary in a mental hospital. She spent all her working life there until ill-health forced her to retire early. Apart from working in the church and playing the piano, which gives her much pleasure, adult education classes have been her main activity. Mrs. C. currently attends classes as part of her routine and at the moment is following the immensely popular Multi-Cultural Fashion Course. Her impressive list of past courses includes:

- voice-training
- advanced sewing
- beadwork
- dress-making
- millinery
- lace-making
- sugar craft
- embroidery.

She is also doing a Diploma in Theology through her church in Leicester and Birmingham. Attending classes, in her own words, brings much variety and zest to her life.

When asked how she first discovered adult education, Mrs C. gave an interesting account of how her tutor recruited her to the Highfields Youth and Community Centre 12 years ago. At the time, she was an adult learner in an FE College, and her current tutor was a student there on a teacher training course. Mrs C. and other black students were receiving very little attention and, despite being on another course, her future tutor observed this and gave them some assistance. She told them about HYCC and how much more welcome they would feel.

It was only a year later, when Mrs C. bumped into her again, that she was reminded about HYCC and the standing invitation to join a class there. She went along, and has been attending the Centre ever since. She has passed on her enthusiasm to a number of friends.

Mrs C. feels that a number of older African-Caribbean people like herself are in need of general education, because their life experiences have not allowed them to make use of what they learnt as young people. She believes that adult education has an important role to play in re-building eroded confidence, particularly if providers begin by finding out what people are good at and encouraging them to build on their talents and abilities.

Mrs C. is planning to return home to Antigua with her mother, and hopes to be able to set up home there and continue to visit her children in Europe, Canada and the USA. Having already made the links in Antigua, she has been asked to help out with some classes there. Providing it does not curb the freedom of movement which her retirement represents, she is hoping to do so. In this way she will be able to continue to pass on to others the skills and knowledge she has gained from her 20 years in adult education.

**AFRICAN-CARIBBEAN ELDERS IN LEICESTER: Individual Case Studies**

**AFRICAN-CARIBBEAN ELDERS IN LEICESTER:** Individual Case Studies

---

**CASE STUDY 2:** Mrs X.

**AGE:** 50+

**STATUS:** Very close to retirement

**NO. OF CHILDREN:** Five

**YEARS IN THE UK:** 32

**COUNTRY OF BIRTH:** Jamaica

---

Like many older African-Caribbean women, Mrs X. waited until her children had finished their education and occupational training before becoming seriously involved in adult education. She describes herself and her husband as being 'behind and beside the children' all the time, and she has not forgotten the obstacles which were placed in their path.

For many years, she was happy to live through her children's successes. They in turn have kept her informed of opportunities and she has made good use of this information. She believes in sharing good news and has made a point of telling her friends about her activities and entreating them to come along too.

Mrs X. received her basic schooling in Jamaica. Her parents very much wanted to put her 'to her books' but she was afraid of academic learning. As soon as she had a choice, she decided to learn sewing instead. Her parents were disappointed, as she was an only child and they were hoping she'd do better for herself. In the event, they supported her choice and allowed her to go off to sewing classes.

By the age of 20, she was an accomplished seamstress, including bridal work, and was teaching younger girls to sew. When she came to England to join her fiancé and to seek better opportunities, she continued sewing and then became a nursing auxiliary. At this point, her inadequate education began to hold her back, and she very much regretted not having taken the opportunity when it had been offered to her.

She subsequently became a wife and mother. Both she and her husband were devoted to their children, and in her words she 'didn't have the heart' to leave them in order to study and better herself.

The only time she did so was to attend a term's basic maths course in order to help her youngest daughter with her homework. That was 20 years ago, and did not continue because the class closed.

Although she is happy for them now, she sometimes wishes she had put some of that determination to better her children's lives into her own education. For example, when two of her daughters did not pass their English 'O' Level exam, she regularly drove them to night classes after working all day and collected them later. Even now, when she is close to retirement, she still regrets that her lack of education prevented her from becoming a Registered General Nurse and advancing her career to a higher level.

Since her children have grown up, Mrs X. has participated in a range of classes. These include:

- maths
- tailoring
- diploma in theology (through her church)
- pattern cutting
- swimming
- youth leadership course (also church-run)
- yoga.

She has also acted as a mentor, supporting other black students in education, and has recently been attending another church-run course entitled 'Black women in the Home, Church and Community'. Even though she would love to improve her maths and English, time is now against her. What with her family, paid employment, church work and the two classes she currently goes to, there is little time left over. However, she is proud to attend a weekly yoga class at a centre where her daughter (who studied art and youthwork) currently works; and she envisages continuing with this and her swimming classes, because of the direct benefit to her health and general fitness.

Mrs X. believes that family networks in the Caribbean community are becoming more established, meaning that more childcare demands are being made, particularly on grandmothers like herself. Her own time management skills are admirable, but she sympathises with those elders who plead shortage of time as a reason for not taking part in any classes.

Her daughters now joke that they cannot stop her. She is quite a role model in the Caribbean community and is used to being interviewed. Although she is still not confident about her grasp of written English – despite having learnt formal English grammar in school back in Jamaica – she is an accomplished speaker in groups and seminars. She is a firm believer in lifelong education, and an advocate and living testimony to the benefits of keeping body and mind alive into old age.

**AFRICAN-CARIBBEAN ELDERS IN LEICESTER: Individual Case Studies**

**CASE STUDY 3:** Mrs Y.

**AGE:** 60+

**STATUS:** Pensioner

**YEARS IN THE UK:** 37

**COUNTRY OF BIRTH:** Jamaica

Mrs Y. came to this country in 1956 to join her husband. She received a basic school education, which she describes as 'formal and positive'. For much of her working life, she has been an residential care assistant, first in an old people's home and subsequently in a children's home. She has also raised a family.

She has been retired for several years now, and leads an active life which includes gardening, catering, housework, church work, looking after her children and grandchildren and attending college. She is presently enrolled on a twice-weekly sewing class, where she is learning to make her own garments and where her current tutor impresses her with her ability to use both English and Asian languages for instruction purposes. Because she is a pensioner, the provision is free, although she has to pay for her own fabrics and thread. She has also done courses in woodwork, computing and assertiveness in the past, but finds her current commitments more than enough. She originally learnt about adult education classes from her sister-in-law.

Had she lived out her retirement in Jamaica, she feels life would be very different for her. She would 'know what to do' and would be able to be 'more creative'. She believes there would probably be more opportunities for someone of her age to find part-time paid employment to supplement her pension.

Mrs Y. is convinced that educational activities like these are very important, especially for older people. In her own words, the classes get them 'out of them home and out of themselves'. She would like to see a lot more African-Caribbean elders being encouraged to participate in adult education, and feels more should be done to advertise the potential benefits to elderly people in her own community. If more classes in Catering, Basic Sewing and Caribbean Cookery were laid on, she thinks this would help.

# Educational Provision for Black Elders in Leicester

- many of the black elders who attend classes other than ESOL have had earlier experiences of adult education and did not need to be convinced of its value
- many black elders have been acting as ambassadors for community education and other services for the elderly, using word of mouth recommendations and established community networks to recruit friends, acquaintances and family members
- in many cases, with the help of providers and adequate resources, black elders have successfully devised and run their own programmes
- many black elders have demonstrated a preference for non-Schedule 2 leisure courses, for 'taster' courses and for others which do not resemble formal education; interest in formal courses and planned activities has tended to be sporadic
- as well as the problems caused by language barriers, refugee elders face the added disadvantage of poverty – most do not receive occupational pensions and have often found activities such as outings too expensive
- taking account of the identified needs and expressed views of clients is seen by most staff as pivotal to the success of their provision
- an expressed willingness to respond to the individual needs of elderly black clients – and a readiness on the part of staff to be open to all their suggestions – is seen as fundamental good practice, however limited the options or funding may be
- vulnerability to funding cuts hangs like a spectre over much of the available provision for elderly black people, and recent reductions in funding have begun to have a detrimental effect, particularly the loss of funding for part-time tutors, transport and other mobile services
- where black elders have been prepared to voice their protest in defence of current provision, it has been successfully – if temporarily – reprieved.

Although it was not possible within the scope of this project to gather comprehensive statistical data in support of each case study, the written and verbal responses resulting from this survey of educational provision for the elderly in Leicester and other parts of the country have provided the basis · for a number of broad conclusions:

- educational activity – both formal and informal – is a consistent feature of current provision and plays a vital therapeutic role in keeping older black people both mentally alert and physically active

- responses to the educational and other needs of black elders have been largely dependent on initiatives taken by members of their own communities, who have been first to identify and meet needs, typically on a voluntary basis

- responses to the educational needs of black elders around the country appear to be piecemeal and to lack a coherent national framework for delivery

- where local authorities, statutory services and voluntary agencies have been prepared to actively involve and consult with members of the black communities, their efforts to meet the needs of the elderly have been largely successful

- the employment of mother-tongue workers and tutors who understand the culture and background of the elders has been an essential factor in the delivery of sensitive and relevant services

- alongside local adult education providers, organisations like Age Concern and Help the Aged are currently playing a vital role in supporting social, education and recreational initiatives for older black people

- projects offering targeted provision are increasingly inhibited by short-term funding arrangements, inadequate premises and anticipated cuts in resources

- there are many elderly black people who remain isolated from mainstream services and available educational provision; the expansion of outreach provision, including funding for home tutors and part-time tutors, is essential if this trend is to be reversed.

CONCLUSIONS

Age Concern/Institute of Gerontology (1992) *Life After Sixty: A profile of Britain's older population.*

Age Concern (Rochdale) and ASHIA (1990) *Time for Action: Consultation document on the needs of Asian elders.*

Bhalla, Anil and Blakemore, Ken (1981) *Elders of the Ethnic Minority Groups,* Birmingham: All Faiths for One Race (1981).

British Refugee Council (1990) *Age in Exile,* Report from a conference held in November 1990 on the Needs of Elderly Refugees.

Castro, Nidia (1990) *Analysis of Activities and Needs of Elderly Refugees in London,* British Refugee Council.

Harrison, Roger (1988) *Learning Later: A handbook for developing education opportunities with older people,* UDACE/Open University.

Kensington and Chelsea Community History Group (1991) *Nice Tastin': Life and food in the Caribbean.*

Morton, Jane (ed.) (1993) *Recent Research on Services for Black and Minority Ethnic Elderly People,* King's College, Institute of Gerontology.

Norman, Alison (1985) *Triple Jeopardy: Growing old in a second homeland,* Centre for Policy on Ageing.

Owen, David (1993) *Ethnic Minorities in Great Britain: Age and gender structure,* University of Warwick Centre for Research in Ethnic Relations.

Robinson, Vaughan (1982) 'The Assimilation of South and East African Asian Immigrants in Britain', in Coleman D.A. (ed.) *Demography of Immigrants & Minority Groups in the United Kingdom,* Academic Press.

Sinclair, Neil M.C. (1993) *The Tiger Bay Story,* Butetown History and Arts Project.

Standing Conference of Ethnic Minority Senior Citizens (1984) *Ethnic Minority Senior Citizens: A first report.*

REFERENCES & FURTHER READING

# APPENDIX

# *1*

# Organisations Contacted

Age Concern, Camden
Age Concern, Hackney
Age Concern, Haringey
Age Concern, Lambeth
Age Concern, Leicester
Age Concern, Metro Rochdale
Age Concern, Newcastle-upon-Tyne
Age Concern, Preston
Age Concern, Westminster
Avalon Community Education Project, Leicester
Belgrave Baheno Asian Women's Centre, Leicester
British Refugee Council
Butetown History and Arts Project, Cardiff
Cardiff Adult Education Service
Cardiff Race Equality Unit
Charles Wootton College, Liverpool
Chinese Centre, Leicester
Eritreans in the UK, Islington
Highfields Youth and Community Centre, Leicester
Kurdish Cultural Centre, Southwark
Latin American Golden Years Project, Brixton
Latin American Third Age Project, Camden
Liverpool Adult Education Service
Liverpool Race Equality Unit
Living History Project, Leicester
Open University, Milton Keynes
The Pepperpot Club, Ladbroke Grove
Rushey Mead Language Centre, Leicester
Somali Elders Project, Liverpool
South Fields Open Workshop, Leicester
Turkish-Cypriot Elders Project, Haringey
University of London, Department of Extra-Mural Studies
University of London, King's College – Institute of
    Gerontology
University of the Third Age, London
University of Warwick, Centre for Research into Ethnic
    Relations
Vietnamese Association, Leicester
Wandsworth Black Elderly Arts Project
Wesley Hall Community Project
Westcotes Open Workshops, South Fields College, Leicester

# APPENDIX

# 2

# The Particular Requirements of Older People in Ethnic Minority Communities

*[Talk delivered at NIACE's 'Educational Opportunities for Older Adults' Conference – 23 May 1993, Westminster Hall, London]*

Before I tell you about the *Older and Wiser* project referred to on today's programme, I'd like to introduce you to three people whom I've come across in the course of the research I've conducted to date.

They are ...

- all 'black' (not in terms of skin-colour but in the political sense – in that they are all potential targets of racism due to their *identifiable* racial, national, ethnic, religious, cultural or linguistic differences)

- all members of 'ethnic minority communities' (i.e. communities of migrant, immigrant, refugee or settler peoples who have found their way to Britain, less often through choice than through necessity, and increasingly nowadays as a result of conditions of political or economic desperation).

**Mrs S.** is a 68-year-old Jamaican woman, a retired primary school teacher who came to this country some 40 years ago in the early 1950s and settled in North Kensington. She was trained as a teacher in the Caribbean, and taught in a local primary school up to her retirement. She is an active member of the local Pentecostal church – and she is now a pensioner.

She attends two luncheon clubs each week, both of which are organised by local churches (Pentecostal and Methodist). The predominantly African-Caribbean clientele provides her with welcome and ongoing social contact and is effectively a network. It is there she learns about any trips to places of interest or coach outings that are on offer; about any courses or activities; and over a Caribbean lunch, she can also take advantage of the local grapevine for news about old friends and acquaintances – the marriages, christenings, ailments, deaths and other happenings in the community. Afterwards, there's dominoes and cards, or (arthritis permitting) basket or rug-making. She is also doing a French course with U3A, and some voluntary home-visiting, organised through her church.

Mrs S. had contacted me initially because she wanted to know if I could tell her of any provision I had come across which offered pursuits which, in her words, were 'more mentally stimulating'. Despite having enrolled with the U3A, she was feeling starved of intellectual discourse, and was wondering if I knew of any African-Caribbean organisations which offered more than the typical diet of dominoes, rice and peas and annual outings to Margate.

In many ways, Mrs S. is typical of a generation of older black people, who came to the UK in the post-war boom years, originally with the intention of returning home, who now finds herself unable or unwilling to do so. In 1983, HMSO published a breakdown of the Census which indicated that there were roughly 16,000 African-Caribbeans of pensionable age, with a further 100,000 over 45s who were due to reach pensionable age in the coming two decades. The 1991 results are still being analysed, but the current figure, even allowing for those who have been able to realise the dream of returning home, is likely to be well over 50,000.

Mrs S. is also typical in that she has been used to an active working life and, having reached retirement age, is keen to find ways of keeping herself busy and keeping her mind alert in the company of others like herself, whom she can relate to both socially and culturally. Despite the diversity of Caribbean cultures, and the tendency of many older people to stick to those from their own island – which she described as the 'small island' mentality of some of her peers – Mrs S. still feels more at home in an environment where the majority of her fellow pensioners are black. As another Caribbean pensioner put it, when interviewed as part of a Nottingham survey, the problem is that 'there are some white people my age group ... who think we shouldn't have the things that are provided for pensioners. They don't even think we should have a bus pass.'

My next introduction is to **Mrs A.**, a Pakistani woman who lives in a residential home in Leicester. Mrs A. is 70 years old, and despite having been here for nearly 20 years, she has had no real opportunity or incentive to learn English. She has spent all her time here living in her son's home, rarely venturing out alone, and there it was sufficient for her to speak Urdu and to learn about the unfamiliar ways of the English from the accounts of her children and grandchildren.

Contrary to the stereotype, however, Mrs A.'s children did not elect to continue to care for her in their home into her old age. There were practical problems resulting from her increasing incontinence and immobility. And there were other, cultural ones which Leicester's Age Concern organiser, Ben Gamadia has described as 'a general loss of status' among Asian elders, resulting from the adoption by younger Asians of Western lifestyles and values. He has found that many younger Asian people are finding that overcrowding in single-family houses and the economic pressure of both partners having to be in full-time work are breaking down the traditional extended family structures, effectively leaving old people like Mrs A. to fend for herself.

Mrs A. was fortunate enough to be given a place in residential care, although changes resulting from the Community Care Act may make such provision less accessible to others like her. The residential project where she lives, funded by Age Concern, gives her access not only to the care she needs, and a diet she is accustomed to, but also to a range of activities and facilities that, had she stayed in her son's home, she would probably never have contemplated.

There's the Leicestershire Living History project, for example, which has set out to record and video Asian elders from all walks of life in their mother-tongue, about their experience of life in Britain and the religious, cultural and social changes they have witnessed in their lifetimes, so that this valuable historical record can be passed on to upcoming and future generations.

There are also social activities, and a language tutor who comes in to the centre to teach those who want to learn English and are brave enough in their latter years to break the web of cultural isolation which is the lot of so many elderly Asian men and women.

A study of the East African and South Asian communities in Blackburn by Vaughan Robinson in 1982 showed that there were 17 distinct minority groups, each with strong individual characteristics, within that overall umbrella – ranging from rural Gujurati Muslims to urban Pakistani Punjabi Muslims; from Punjabi Sikhs to East African Gujurati Hindus; Bengalis, and others. These cultural, linguistic and religious differences have huge implications for education and other service providers, and are compounded by differences between those who arrived here in the earlier waves of immigration in the 50s and 60s and those who came later, as a result of expulsions and political upheaval.

So, despite the fact that Mrs A. may be typical of many women of her generation, her needs are very specific. For her counterparts in other parts of the country, where Asian settlement has been more sparse, there continues to be very little available provision and Leicester appears to be the exception rather than the rule.

My third introduction is to **Amada Vergara**. A Chilean refugee, she came here in the 1970s, post-Allende, along with many of her compatriots who had been tortured and forced to live in exile by the new Pinochet regime. Based in Brixton, she has set up a group called the Latin American Golden Years club. Working with Latin American refugees like herself of 55 or over, she offers individual and group counselling, art therapy, craft classes, social and cultural events and a regular meeting place where they can talk, reminisce and watch Spanish-language films together. She has no formal training, and literally goes to the library one day to read up on what she may be required to teach the next. When I asked her about funding, she laughed. A bric-a-brac stall she runs on a Saturday morning and periodic raffles bring in sufficient money for art materials and other basic necessities. The rest comes from her own pocket.

When I asked her about her counselling skills, and mentioned the possibility of getting formal training, she replied that she was reluctant to mention this need on any funding application because it would be selfish on her part, and might give a false impression of dependency.

Amada may not be typical among volunteers, but those she caters for are representative of many thousands of elderly refugees who have, particularly since the late 80s, come here from different corners of the globe – Somalians, Ethiopians, Kurds, Ugandans, Eritreans, Vietnamese and others – who face similar situations and have a common experience of trauma, uprooting, isolation and language barriers.

I have chosen to focus on these three women for several reasons: firstly, because they **all present a challenge to common**

**stereotypes** about provision for the black elderly. Mrs S., with her refusal to accept brain-death; Afshan, forced to live outside the extended family and cope with institutional life; and Amada, self-reliant, multi-skilled and totally in-tune with her own people's needs.

Secondly, they are **all black women**, and it is well known that women's greater longevity means that, as the older members of the different black communities begin to come of age, it is likely to be women, more so than men, who will be in need of particular forms of sheltered housing, social, health, welfare and education provision. Warwick University is currently analysing the 1991 census data regarding age and ethnicity, and I have not seen the results yet, but the 1987–89 Labour Force Survey indicated that roughly 5% of black/ethnic minority people are over 60, with a further 13% between 45–59. With a total black and ethnic minority population in the UK of approximately 5.5m, we are looking at a potential 600,000 elders with needs that have thus far remained largely unmet.

I also chose to talk about these women because they typify the diversity of needs and circumstances among black elders – and the commonalities.

For example, the fact that they have **all grown old in this country**, and, regardless of friends and family ties, are still relegated to the status of strangers, cut off from their original homeland and, in many ways, from the younger generations in their own communities who have been raised here and may have become Westernised and culturally estranged.

The fact, too, of their **collective vulnerability to social isolation**, particularly where language barriers or cultural requirements have been a factor; exacerbated by the shared frustrations of those who are illiterate, housebound, infirm, disabled, sight- or hearing-impaired, or speakers of little or no English.

Above all, there is their **common need for a social, educational and cultural forum** where they can be with people with whom, as Alison Norman (author of *Triple Jeopardy*) puts it, 'communication is instinctive, and ... jokes, means of relaxation, fears, hopes and problems are part of a common unspoken language arising from life experience ...'

Much of the good practice I have become aware of to date has been in the voluntary sector, and there are some exciting examples of innovation – **oral history and reminiscence projects** offering elders a chance to record their life histories through a variety of media; **mobile libraries**, offering mother-tongue literature; cultural initiatives – one Latin American group of pensioners based in Camden participates in **international festivals**, performing dance/folk music; one group of Vietnamese pensioners, who share premises with a Vietnamese youth club, participate in **story-telling,** allowing them to pass on to the youth a knowledge of traditional festivals, beliefs and folk-tales.

Most education services are only now beginning to recognise the needs of pensioners, much less the very specific needs of elderly black people. **Pre-retirement courses**, in particular, are becoming more common, and although I know of no such courses targeted specifically at black elders, attempts are being made by some colleges and WEA branches to recruit from black communities by means of the ethnic press and targeted publicity translated into community languages. **Efforts to provide for the visually or hearing impaired, and moves to improve wheelchair access** are also likely to provide a greater incentive to older adults, both white and black, to take up educational opportunities in colleges.

Adult education courses that have traditionally attracted older black people – particularly art, craft and cookery, and other creative activities – are of course threatened by **new funding criteria** (Schedule 2). A lot of important work is going on at present in individual projects around the country, often funded by the local adult education service which provides tutors or funding for part-time hours. Like many other groups in our communities, black elders stand to lose out if non-vocational courses become full-cost or are deemed unviable due to changed funding priorities. There are of course many exceptional examples of black pensioners who have opted for mainstream vocational courses, and I've no doubt that Adult Learners' Week will highlight more, as in previous years.

The preferred and most effective model of adult education provision for the black elderly appears to be **outreach** – sending tutors into residential homes, religious, community and day care centres to provide ESOL, keep-fit, craft, welfare rights and other classes. This may be particularly at risk, since outreach is costly in terms of staff time and travel and the resources needed to provide a proper service.

I still have a way to go before this research project is completed, but let me sum up what I have learnt to date. It is clear that:

- demographic changes highlight the fact that the need for educational opportunities for older black adults is likely to increase drastically over the next decade and pose an increasing challenge to all involved
- the demand from all groups is great (and largely unmet); existing provision is piecemeal and needs a more coherent national framework for delivery
- there are a number of examples of good practice around the country, and a lot can be learnt from their successes and set-backs – in particular, some interesting partnerships (for example, between Age Concern and ethnic minority housing associations, local authorities and community volunteers, etc.). I hope, in my report, to highlight some of these to show how creative resourcing and funding can benefit black elders in a practical, meaningful way
- above all, I have learnt something about ageism. Racism is a hurdle in its own right, but when coupled with assumptions that, because of age, a person's ability to learn or their desire to improve the quality of their lives will be curtailed, it becomes a huge and very daunting barrier. The losers are not only the old people themselves, whose experience, skills, resourcefulness and knowledge are undermined by such attitudes. By implication, we all lose by allowing such an invaluable human resource to remain untapped.

# APPENDIX

# *3*

# Questionnaires

# QUESTIONNAIRE FOR PROVIDERS

The purpose of this questionnaire is to identify good educational practice and/or innovative provision for black/ethnic minority elders, whether of a formal kind or informal kind. If possible, the questions should be completed by the Project Co-ordinator or a Tutor who is directly involved in the provision.

## 1. PROJECT DETAILS

Name: _____

Address: _____

_____

_____

Tel. no: _____

Project aims: _____

Target group: _____

Funding
source(s): _____

Project description (please tick and/or describe, as appropriate):

☐ Adult Education  ☐ Voluntary organisation  ☐ Housing Association

☐ Community Centre  ☐ Religious organisation  ☐ Other *(please describe)*

_____

## 2. What activities, if any, do you offer which cater specifically for the needs or interests of elders in the local black/ethnic minority communities?

*(If none, which existing activities tend to attract them and why?)*

*Appendix 3 (a)*

**3. Did you identify a need for this kind of provision, or were you responding to a need that was identified by others?**
*(If so, by whom?)*

**4. Was the provision set up by your organisation alone, or in partnership with other agencies?**

**5. How do you publicise it?**

**6. Do you receive any additional outside assistance with funding/resources/transport/publicity, etc?**

**7. What constraints or hurdles have you encountered, if any, in catering for black/ethnic minority elders?**

**8. Are there any improvements you would like to be able to make to the programme/activities you offer them?**

**9. What are the project's best features/greatest successes?**

**10. What are the project's worst features/major drawbacks?**

**11. What other educational/social/cultural needs do black/ethnic minority elders in your community have which remain unmet?**

**12. In you had to advise others on how to go about setting up and running a similar project/educational activity for black/ethnic minority elders, what would you identify as essential good practice?**
*(please list)*

**13. Are there any resource implications which they would have to take on?**
*(i.e. what would they need in order to do it properly?)*

**14. Can you sum up what individual black/ethnic minority clients gain from the project/activity?**

# QUESTIONNAIRE FOR CLIENTS

Where possible, these questions should be completed in the course of an informal personal interview, if necessary with the assistance of a mother-tongue interpreter, allowing as much time as possible for response to be explored or supplemented.

## 1. What is your ...

Name:

Age:

Nationality:

Gender:

Ethnic origin:

Family status *(i.e. single/married/living with children/ widowed*, etc.):

First language/ mother-tongue:

## 2. How long have you lived in this country?

## 3. What were your reasons for coming to live here?

## 4. How would you describe the education you've received?
*(i.e. was it formal/informal? basic/advanced? positive/negative? etc.)*

*Appendix 3 (b)*

**5. What job or profession did you have before you retired?**

**6. How do you spend your time now you are retired?**
*(i.e. what does your typical day/week look like?)*

**7. Are you involved in any educational activities?**
*(i.e. anything that involves an element of learning)*
*If so, can you describe what you do?*

**8. Who organises the activity/activities?**
*What language(s) does the tutor/group leader use?*

**9. How did you find out about the provision?**

**10. Is it specially for elders?**
*(i.e. people of post-retirement age)*

**11. Is it specially for elders from black/ethnic minority communities?**
*If so, which one(s)?*

**12. How often do you attend?**
*(Do you need to use any form of transport in order to get there?)*

**13. Is it free?**
*(If not, what fees/expenses do you have to cover for yourself?)*

**14. Are there any other educational activities you would like to be able to do?** *(What prevents you from doing them?)*

**15. If you had to make a list of your educational needs – or the needs of people like yourself from a similar age-group and background – what would you say they are?**

**16. If you had to advise someone on how to organise an activity to meet any of these needs – or if you were able to do it yourself – what would be the best way of going about it?**
*(i.e. who would you get to pay for it? where would it take place? how would you get people to come along? what sort of things would they do?)*

**17. If someone asked you to help out with an educational programme for young people in your community – for example in a school, community centre or youth club – what would you be able to contribute?**

**18. If you were living out your retirement in your country of origin, how would your life be different?**

NOTES